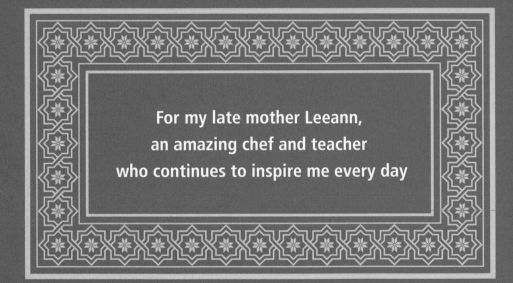

For my late mother Leeann,
an amazing chef and teacher
who continues to inspire me every day

Everyday Thai Cooking

QUICK AND EASY FAMILY STYLE RECIPES

KATIE CHIN

Foreword by KATIE WORKMAN

Photography by MASANO KAWANA

TUTTLE Publishing

Tokyo | Rutland, Vermont | Singapore

Summer Rolls with Shrimp and Mint

Lemongrass Chicken Wings

Contents

Green Papaya Crab Salad

Sour Spicy Shrimp Soup

Shaking Beef

A Cookbook to Treasure...

Thai food is as exciting as it gets. I won't try to encapsulate why, because Katie Chin has done a wonderful job of presenting it, but suffice it to say that when Katie told me she was writing a Thai cookbook, a pleasurable little shock went through me. I can't quite dissect which part was the pure pleasure of thinking about Thai food, or which was the thrill of knowing that Katie was tackling the subject.

The words Katie Chin uses to open her cookbook, to describe Thai food, are wonderfully analogous to the words I would use to describe her: Bold. Exotic. Diverse. Pungent. Sweet. Sour. Salty, Hot. Crunchy. Bright. Fragrant. Soothing. Unique. Alive.

Actually, the only words I skipped are "sometimes bitter," as I haven't known that to be the case with Katie. But really, would that be so bad?

I know you want to hear about the recipes. And you should; they are fantastic. But first a bit of background.

I met Katie Chin when she and her famous restaurateur mom pitched a book to me when I was a cookbook editor. Katie was in the supporting role to her mom, who was a Chinese restaurateur against all odds, immigrating from China with her husband to Minneapolis, starting a tailoring business to make ends meet, cooking a "thank you dinner" for her clients, which led to teaching cooking classes, which led to catering, which led to a collection of successful Asian restaurants. Leeann was a quiet powerhouse of a woman, and Katie was filled with admiration for her mom, and a more than willing student. We both learned together during the making of that book.

Katie then became a caterer, and a cookbook author in her own right, and her great skill is taking authentic Asian food and translating it into something deliciously accessible for our modern pantries and kitchens. That she has tackled Thai food, one of the most popular and delicious Asian cuisines, in this book will make many of us very happy.

Segue to the recipes! The condiment chapter alone knocked my socks off. I want to add Nam Prik Pao to everything I eat from this day forward. My family and neighbors adored the Thai Flat Noodles (Rad Na), and the lemongrass chicken wings were stupidly finger-licking delicious. I have now stocked up on tamarind and galangal and of course ginger, garlic, and fish sauce, and am expecting this cookbook to join the splattered, battered ranks of favorite cookbooks in my kitchen.

It's always exciting to bring a new cuisine into your comfort zone. Being able to recreate the fresh, bright, and addicting flavors of Thai food in my own kitchen is a joy, and I am going to think of Katie with gratitude with every Gai Yaang that graces my table.

KATIE WORKMAN

The Joys of Thai Cooking

Bold. Exotic. Diverse. Pungent. Sweet. Sour. Salty. Hot. Sometimes bitter. Crunchy. Bright. Fragrant. Soothing. Unique. Alive. All these words and more come to mind when I think of Thai food.

My love affair with Thai food began when I was in high school growing up in Minnesota under the tutelage of my famous chef/restaurateur mother, Leeann Chin. I grew up learning the fundamentals of Chinese cuisine: stir-frying, steaming, grilling, deep-frying, creating velvety sauces and intricate dumplings. My culinary worldview was a Cantonese one.

Then one day that all changed. My mother took me to Arun's Gourmet Thai Restaurant in Chicago when we went to visit my brother, Bill, who was earning his PhD in mathematics and, suddenly, my taste buds exploded with aromatic essences, piquant flavors, and abundant textures from our eight-course meal.

Chinese cuisine has had a major influence on Thai cooking. The threads of Chinese techniques and flavors are ever so delicately woven into Thai dishes that I felt an homage to my Chinese heritage with each bite. I was impassioned by the exciting flavors I was experiencing: my first sip of Tom Yum Soup, the crunch of the roasted rice powder in the Larb, the spike of chilies in the Chicken with Thai Chili and Basil and the sour, sweet tangy satisfaction from my first taste of Pad Thai. Finally, the cooling sensation of a mango shake tempered the thrill of culinary sensations I was encountering for the first time.

After leaving my career as a film and television marketing executive to follow my culinary dreams, I formed Double Happiness Catering and was excited to put my love of bold and exotic Thai flavors to the test in my pan-Asian catering kitchen. Soon I was mincing lemongrass for Thai steamed mussels, simmering large pots of Thai curries and threading pounds of chicken for satays with spicy peanut sauce. My clients went wild and my culinary world view was forever broadened.

Chiang Mai Chicken in Lettuce Cups

Grilled Fresh Salmon with Green Curry Sauce

Being aware of my love for Thai food, my husband whisked me off to Thailand for our honeymoon. What an amazing guy! We set forth on our culinary odyssey with open hearts, minds, and palates. We strolled around Bangkok sampling all that Thai street food has to offer, from satays and crispy spring rolls to steaming bowls of noodles and Som Yum Salad. We rented a jeep and traveled along the Mae Hong Son Pass from Chiang Mai sampling this region's famous Burmese style cooking. We traveled over to the Northeastern province of Issan where we sampled melt-in-your-mouth Shaking Beef (page 81) and delicate rice paper summer rolls influenced by the Vietnamese immigrant population. Heading south, we spent the tail end of our trip island hopping to Phuket, Koh Samui, Pi Pi, and Krabi. There, we were treated to seafood that was so fresh it felt like it was jumping onto our plates from the sea—from crispy whole fish topped with spicy garlic-chili sauces to tender clams simmering in a delicious and pungent chili basil sauce. I came back with a full belly, tons of new ideas, and an excited heart eager to take my love of Thai cooking to the next level.

I retired from my catering business to become a mom to twins, Dylan and Becca and stepdaughter Kyla. As a new mother, I related to my friends who lamented about how challenging it is to get dinner on the table. Tired of takeout, all of my friends were begging me for new recipe ideas so I created my blog, *The Sweet and Sour Chronicles* where I share my knowledge, tips, and recipes for creating everyday Asian dishes.

When I was asked to write *Everyday Thai Cooking*, I jumped at the chance. I'm excited to arm you with my collection of Thai recipes for real people who are juggling hectic schedules. My book will show you how simple and economical Thai cooking can truly be, and soon, you'll be weaving your own brilliant Thai tapestries of taste, texture, and aroma. You'll soon develop a love affair with Thai cooking too. Not only will you be the talk of the neighborhood, but you can kiss your take-out menus goodbye.

Katie Chin

KATIE CHIN

Basic Cooking Techniques and Tips

Thai cooking is much easier than you think. Yup, it's true. When I gathered a group of friends for an impromptu Thai cooking class at my house the other day, they couldn't believe how simple and quick it was to make. "Are you kidding me? It takes longer for take-out to get to my door and the restaurant is less than a mile away." Thai cooks pride themselves on simplicity of technique. At its very core, Thai cooking is about using the freshest ingredients, with an emphasis on aromatic herbs and spices, to achieve a balance of hot, sweet, sour, and salty flavors in every dish. In fact, the actual cooking time for most Thai dishes is 15 to 30 minutes! With a couple of exceptions, it's all about fast cooking at high heat levels and using interesting herbs and spices, usually at the beginning and end of cooking. Okay, it's time to throw out those take-out menus and follow these simple, no-fail rules for healthier, tastier, and easier Thai meals at home. Ready, set, go!

HOW TO PREPARE LEMONGRASS

Preparing lemongrass is important because you will use it all the time when cooking Thai food. It's easy to understand why this frisky cousin to ginger, with its citrusy aroma and woodsy-lemony flavor, is widely used in Thai cooking—it enhances every dish it touches.

There are two ways to prepare lemongrass: Finely chopped for marinades, stir-fries, salads and curries; and cut into larger pieces for soups and sauces.

HOW TO MINCE LEMONGRASS

1. Remove the first 4–5 tough fibrous outer layers of the lemongrass stalk with your fingers to reveal the softer, yellower part of the stalk that you'll be using. The remaining layers will still be slightly fibrous.
2. Using a sharp, serrated knife, slice off the bulb (bottom 2 inches/5 cm) and discard.
3. Now, using the back of a knife, oblong pestle, or rolling pin (or a wine bottle if that's all you have), smash the bottom 6 inches (15 cm) of the lemongrass stalk to release the essential oils and separate the fibers.
4. Next, use a sharp knife and finely chop the bottom 1/3 of the stalk.

HOW TO CHOP LEMONGRASS IN YOUR FOOD PROCESSOR AND FREEZE FOR LATER USE

To save time, I like to prepare a large quantity of lemongrass and freeze it so I can just grab some from the freezer. I usually buy at least 4 pounds and follow these simple steps:

1. Follow steps #1 and #2 from How to Mince Lemongrass. Next, slice off the green, fibrous parts of the stalk at the top with a sharp serrated knife. Feed the bulb ends through the food processor blade until sliced. Remove the sliced lemongrass and mince by hand.
2. Place minced lemongrass in a quart-sized resealable plastic food-storage bag, about 1/2 cup (50 g) per bag, and flatten. Once frozen, break off whatever you need for future recipes and return the rest to the freezer.

HOW TO PREPARE LEMONGRASS FOR SOUPS AND SAUCES

1. Follow steps #1 and #2 from How to Mince Lemongrass. Next, slice off the green, fibrous parts of the stalk at the top with a sharp serrated knife. Now, smash the remaining stalk to release the essential oils. Cut the stalk into 1-inch (2.5 cm) or 2-inch (5 cm) pieces depending on the recipes directions.

HOW TO SLICE THAI CHILIES

Thai chilies are among the hottest on the planet (50,000–100,000 on the Scoville heat scale!) so it's important that you use a latex, rubber glove on one hand while slicing these hot-tempered babies. Remember to slice finely (unless otherwise noted in the recipe), so your guests or family don't place a large piece in their mouth inadvertently. As noted in the recipes, feel free to deseed Thai chilies or use a milder chili if you prefer less heat. If cooking for young children, you can select a milder chili or omit altogether.

DEEP-FRYING TIPS AND TRICKS

Deep-frying in Thai cooking usually involves batter-dipped pieces of meat or fish or the frying of appetizers or desserts wrapped in flour-based or rice-based skins, like spring rolls. Deep-frying requires very high heat levels (350°F to 375°F /175°C to 190C°). Make sure the oil isn't too hot, because food will overcook on the outside and will be undercooked on the inside. It isn't necessary to use a wok when deep-frying but you must always use a deep pan to adequately cover the items you are frying. For example, if you are using 2 inches (5 cm) of oil, you must leave 6 inches (15 cm) of space above the oil. If your oil begins smoking, turn off the heat for a few minutes and let the oil return to 350°F (175C°). Heat oil uncovered to prevent overheating.

Also, if the temperature is too low, then the items will soak up too much oil. Don't try to fry too many pieces at one time or the oil temperature will dip. It's also important that anything you deep-fry is dried completely, especially before you dip items into batter or marinade.

Use a deep fat frying thermometer if you have one. If you don't have one, the oil is ready when a 1-inch (2.5 cm) cube of white bread dropped browns after 1 minute in the oil.

I prefer using vegetable oil or corn oil for deep-frying because they have "high smoke points," meaning they don't break down at deep-frying temperatures. In other words, don't use olive oil to deep-fry.

HOW TO MASTER THAI STIR-FRYING

Thai stir-frying happens very fast, so it's really, REALLY important to be organized and have all of your prep done in advance. Please read each recipe carefully so you'll see if you need to blanch a certain vegetable before it gets thrown into your wok or pan. Blanching preserves the vibrant color of vegetables and cuts down on cooking time. Some vegetables take longer than others so blanching is an important step but you don't want to be caught with your pants down in the middle of a stir-fry.

I recommend arranging all of your ingredients on a tray in the order in which they'll be used. If it helps, you can number each ingredient. I make my twins help make numbered cards so they feel like they're helping and it does really help when I'm making several courses for a dinner party. Also have all of your tools ready to go and in the order you'll be using them.

It's also important to allow the wok or pan to heat up first before adding the oil, swirling to coat. The wok or pan is ready when a drop of water cast on the surface sizzles and evaporates immediately. I recommend using a non-stick wok or frying pan as you'll need less oil, and protein is less likely to stick to the pan. Ensure that your frying pan has high walls so the ingredients don't fly out.

When stir-frying, you must use a firm spatula which will easily slide under the ingredients. Don't try to "stir" the food! I know, it's a bit of a misnomer. Instead, try to slip the spatula under the food, folding over, and then tossing it quickly.

To save time, I like to purchase my stir-fry veggies from the salad bar at my local grocery store where everything is clean and pre-cut. This also cuts down on waste especially when you're cooking for one or two people.

THE SECRET TO FLUFFY RICE (EVERYTIME, AND I'M NOT TALKING ABOUT THE KIND FROM A BOX)

Growing up in a Chinese-American household, I was accustomed to eating long-grain white rice until I discovered jasmine rice as an adult and what a discovery it was! This fragrant cousin to long-grain white rice, also known as Thai fragrant rice, cooks up fluffy, moist, slightly sticky and has a delicious and subtle nutty aroma...If you know how to cook it properly.

The secret to perfectly cooked rice is to wash it first. That's right, wash your rice. This eliminates excess starch from the grains that makes rice mushy.

Fill a pot with the desired rice amount and cool water. Swirl the water around with your hands and wash the rice by rubbing it gently between your fingers; drain. Repeat this process until the water runs clear, usually about 5 or 6 times.

HOW TO COOK A PERFECT POT OF RICE

In a medium, heavy-bottomed pot with a tight-fitting lid, combine 1 cup (185 g) of jasmine rice and 1½ cups (375 ml) of water. Bring to a boil over high heat. As soon as the water is boiling, lower the heat to a simmer and cover. Cook at a gentle simmer until the water is completely absorbed and the rice is tender, about 12 minutes. Remove from the heat and let sit for 10 minutes with a lid on before serving. One cup of raw rice will yield 3 cups (450 g) of cooked rice.

If you're using a rice cooker, wash the rice in the rice cooker bowl. Follow your instruction manual to cook using the 1 cup (185 g) raw rice to 1½ cups (375 ml) water ratio for Thai jasmine rice.

DICING AND CHOPPING IN THAI COOKING

Unlike Chinese cooking, Thai cooking is all about diversity, texture, and rustic appeal. So when a recipe calls for dicing, don't worry so much about uniformity when dicing or chopping for a stir-fry or a salad.

TIPS ON STEAMING

I prefer to use a bamboo steamer when cooking Thai food, but any steamer will do. You can actually improvise in a pinch by placing two empty tuna fish cans to raise a platter 2 inches (5 cm) above the water. Always make sure there's enough water in the pot so it doesn't evaporate when you walk away (I've learned this lesson the hard way a few times, hence the charred bamboo steamers sitting in my garage). Always make sure that the water comes to a rolling boil before steaming and use a secure lid. Line your steamer basket with cabbage or banana leaves to prevent sticking.

RICE NOODLE TIPS

After softening noodles with water, they must be kept moist or they will turn hard. Cover them with plastic wrap or a damp towel if you're not going to use them right away. You can also soak them in water and refrigerate for up to two days.

Basic Tools and Utensils

When I started cooking Thai food, I was pleasantly surprised to find that I had most of the tools and utensils in my kitchen already. If you cook Asian food at home, you probably have most of the tools necessary to cook Thai food too. Simplicity applies not only to the techniques but also to the tools used in Thai cooking. If you stop and think about the amazing meals that street vendors create in Thailand with hardly any space or equipment. Or the millions of Thai people living in rustic dwellings in the country where a burner on the porch serves as the kitchen, it occurs to you how their minimalist approach to cooking applies to the whole process. That said, here's a primer on the basic tools and utensils I think you need to make Thai food at home including some modern inventions for convenience.

WOK, STIR-FRY PAN OR SKILLET

A wok is central to Thai cooking like most Asian cuisines. It's incredibly versatile and used for everything from stir-frying and deep-frying to steaming and braising. Woks are extremely efficient as they heat up quickly and their concave shape allows the pan's surface to become evenly heated with a minimal amount of oil.

There are two types of woks: Cast iron and carbon steel. Carbon steel woks are most readily available. Cast iron woks tend to retain heat better but either is a solid choice. The most user-friendly size is 14 inches (29 cm) in diameter. Look for a wok with sturdy handles and a lid. Woks with rounded bottoms are best for gas stoves as the flames can travel up the sides for even heat distribution. A flat-bottom wok is preferable for electric stoves. Chinese cast iron woks need to be "seasoned." This means the wok has been put through a process of warming, cooling down, and oiling to prevent it from rusting and giving it overall protection. If you season your wok properly, a natural non-stick surface will be created and it will turn dark black.

Here's how to season your cast iron wok:
1 Wash the wok in hot water with a green scouring pad. Dry thoroughly with a paper towel.

2 Heat the wok on high heat. Tilt and turn the wok until it becomes a yellowish-blueish color. Remove from the heat.
3 Using a paper towel, wipe the inside of the wok with a small amount of vegetable oil.
4 Turn the heat to medium-low. Place the wok on the burner for 10 minutes.

Wipe with a fresh paper towel. There will be black residue on he paper towel. Repeat steps #3 and #4 about three times, or until there is no longer black residue on the paper towel when wiped.

If you don't have a wok or you can't remember where you put the one you got for Christmas 10 years ago, you can make all of the recipes in this book with a frying pan or skillet. Just make sure you use a frying pan or skillet with high edges or else the ingredients will fly out of your pan. I like to use a non-stick skillet because you need less oil, and meat won't stick as much. Just make sure to use a non-stick spatula to avoid scratching the non-stick surface of the pan.

For deep-frying and steaming, I like to use an electric wok that I can place in a separate area of my kitchen and provides extra space if I'm also stir-frying or braising a separate dish on my stovetop.

CUTTING BOARD Quality cutting boards are vital to Thai cooking. As with all styles of cooking, I like to keep a separate cutting board for meat proteins and one for fruits, vegetables, and breads. Invest in one large sturdy cutting board for all the chopping, mincing, and dicing in Thai cooking. I use both a bamboo cutting board and plastic cutting boards. I feel that bamboo cutting boards are superior to other cutting boards because they're made from sustainable material which makes them eco-friendly plus they're often made from laminated strips of bamboo so they don't absorb as much water or odors and are less prone to warping.

KNIVES With all the mincing, chopping, and dicing in Thai cooking, invest in quality knives and keep them sharp. A standard 8-inch (20 cm) chef's knife should do the trick along with some paring knives.

You may also want to consider a Chinese cleaver because it's extremely versatile: it slices, it dices, it shreds, it pounds, and it minces! I remember my late mother wielding her cleaver to hack chicken bones for stock and watching it dance across our wooden chopping block as she made cloves of garlic into finely minced pieces.

When shopping for knives or a Chinese cleaver, choose the stainless steel kind as carbon steel is susceptible to rust. It should feel firm and sturdy in your hand but not weigh you down.

MORTAR AND PESTLE A mortar and pestle is used in Thai cooking to pulverize and smash aromatic herbs with other ingredients to make fragrant pastes. A small food processor or blender will do in most cases but you will need a mortar and pestle to make the classic Green Papaya Crab Salad (page 59) where you smash the papaya and green beans. It's one of those recipes where there's nothing like the real thing, baby. It's also used to smash and grind dry toasted rice for the Spicy Thai Salad with Minced Pork (page 54). I also use the pestle to smash lemongrass for soups. Look for a traditional heavy, large Thai mortar and pestle or kroke made of granite.

RICE COOKER I love my rice cooker like I love my dog. It's obedient, doesn't talk back and loves me unconditionally. All this, plus the added benefit of cooking rice perfectly every time. Rice cookers can sense through an internal temperature sensor when boiling water has been absorbed by the rice or grains in the pot. It automatically turns off or switches to warm when this happens which results in fluffy, perfect rice every time. This means you don't have watch it or worry about it burning. We could all use one less thing to have to think about! They take up little space on are easy to clean, especially if you purchase one with non-stick bowl.

There are several models available from $10 up to $500+. The higher priced models have fuzzy logic technology which is a like a rice cooker with a brain able to calibrate the temperature and water quantity for a superior end product. Fuzzy logic machines really do make the best rice I've ever had in my life. I recommend Zojurishi and Cuisinart fuzzy logic rice cooker brands. For the recipes in this book, you can use any method to cook rice, but I recommend getting a rice cooker because you'll use it all of the time especially the jasmine rice.

STRAINER OR SLOTTED SPOON I recommend a traditional Chinese style strainer (spider strainer) with a long bamboo handle. It's made out of wire mesh and is great for removing deep-fried foods from oil as well as removing blanched foods from boiling water. You can find this type of strainer at an Asian market or specialty gourmet stores. It's an indispensable tool in my kitchen. You can also use a wide, western-style slotted spoon in place of a Chinese style strainer.

SPATULA When using a wok, I recommend using a Chinese steel spatula, wooden spatula or a heavy duty plastic, non-stick spatula. You want a heavy duty tool when stir-frying because you will be tossing and flipping ingredients quickly and you want to ensure even cooking.

If you're using a non-stick frying pan, stick with a wooden or non-stick plastic spatula. It's a good idea to have your tools laid out before you start cooking. If you're cooking a multi-course meal, make sure you have a spatula ready for each stir-fry dish.

LEMON/LIME SQUEEZER Many Thai recipes call for freshly squeezed lime juice so it's a good idea to have a manual or electric lemon/lime squeezer. In a pinch, you can buy store-bought lime juice, but nothing beats the real thing. My mother taught me to press and roll limes on a counter with your hand a few times before juicing to get the most juice.

LATEX SURGICAL GLOVES Capsaicin, is the compound in the hot chilies responsible for the heat. It's important to wear latex, surgical gloves while handling or cutting hot chilies or else the capsaicin residue while burn your skin and is especially painful if you touch your eyes, nostrils, or mouth. It's even more important if you have small children in your home as you don't want to accidentally touch their eyes or skin after handling hot chilies without wearing gloves. I buy a large box and keep them in my pantry so they're always on hand (pun intended).

FOOD PROCESSOR I say, keep life simple. A food processor makes life a lot easier for blending salad dressings, blending pastes such as roasted red chili paste, grating papaya, chopping lemongrass—oh, I could go on and on. As with lemongrass, I like to mince large quantities of ginger in advance and freeze it for later use.

There are many models available at affordable price points. I recommend buying a standard model and as well as a small food processor to blend pastes. Get the attachment blades so you can grate carrots, papaya, and other veggies in a snap.

Understanding Thai Ingredients

Thai cooking is all about creating contrasts from the hot and sour to the sweet and pungent to the spicy and fragrant using a combination of core ingredients. When I asked my Minneapolis-based sister, Laura, to test one of the recipes for this book, I was delighted to hear that she could find everything she needed for the recipe at her local grocery store. Times have really changed since the days when we couldn't even find fresh ginger at our neighborhood supermarket growing up in the Midwest. With the soaring popularity of Asian cooking, many grocery stores or specialty stores carry the basic Thai ingredients you will need to cook everyday Thai food. In some cases, you may need to make a trip your local Asian market (bring the kids because it is always a fun adventure). If you don't live in an area with an Asian market, there are several on-line ethnic specialty food resources (page 140). Once again, simplicity is the key theme in Thai cooking so it isn't difficult to keep main pantry items on hand with your dishes ultimately coming alive with fresh vegetables, aromatic herbs, and proteins.

Bamboo shoots are the part of a bamboo plant that is harvested before it matures. The edible part is the tender cream-colored meat inside the shoot. Large shoots are often sliced and added to curries. Smaller shoots can be eaten whole as a dish onto themselves, either cooked or pickled. Available fresh, canned or bottled, bamboo shoots are found in Asian markets and many grocery stores.

Banana leaves make a beautiful and aromatic wrap for foods like rice, fish, and meat. The long, waxy leaves transfer some of their subtle grassy aroma to any food wrapped within them. Before using banana leaves, they should be placed in hot water or carefully held over a flame for a few seconds to make them more pliable. If you can't find banana leaves, use lotus or large cabbage leaves, or, the old stand-by, aluminum foil. The leaves are often sold frozen in Asian and Latin markets. I buy a few packs at a time to have on hand in my freezer. They're great for dressing up platters when entertaining.

Basil (Thai and holy) is an essential ingredient in Thai cooking and is used throughout this book. Thai basil and holy basil are the two most commonly used varieties of basil in Thai cooking. Thai, or Asian, is a tropical variety with a strong peppery, anise flavor that stands up really well to cooking. It has purple flowers, red-tinged stems, and pointy green leaves. Holy basil is so named because it is held sacred in the Hindu culture. It is revered in Thai cooking for its subtle, minty flavor that comes alive when heated. When buying either variety, choose bunches that are fresh, fragrant, and show no signs of wilting. Separate the leaves from the stems and wash and dry them well before use. A substitute for either variety is fresh Italian basil (the kind found in most supermarkets). Italian basil isn't quite as fragrant or flavorful as Thai or holy basil so you may want to add a bit more.

Black mushrooms Also known as dried shiitakes or fragrant mushrooms, black mushrooms are incredibly versatile. When dried black mushrooms are presoaked in water they plump up and have a deliciously meaty taste and texture. Strain the water used to soak the mushrooms and add it to dishes to add even more flavor to stir-fries, soups, rice dishes, and curries.

Coconut milk Slightly sweet and creamy with a light jasmine aroma, coconut milk is a popular ingredient in Thai cooking. It adds richness and flavor to curries, sauces, soups, desserts, and drinks. Made by pressing fresh coconut flesh, the first pressing produces thick, creamy coconut cream, and subsequent pressings produce thinner, yet still creamy, coconut milk. It is widely available in cans. Choose an un-sweetened variety and shake it well because it will have separated in the can. Coconut milk is widely available and available at most grocery stores. It's also great for lactose-free diets.

Fresh coriander leaves (cilantro) Also known as Chinese parsley, coriander leaves are one of the most popular fresh herbs in the world and are used throughout the recipes in this book. Its refreshingly spicy, citrusy flavor tempers the heat in many Thai dishes. Whether chopped to release its maximum flavor or left whole, coriander leaves are best enjoyed raw and added just before serving a cooked dish. Fresh coriander leaves, seeds, and stems are also important ingredients in Thai cuisine. The seeds are coriander, a spice that is an ingredient in some Thai dishes. The stems have a strong peppery aroma, which makes them a popular addition to curry paste and homemade stocks.

Curry pastes The most common ingredients in curry pastes include chilies, garlic, galangal, and lemongrass, which are ground together into an intensely aromatic paste. What gives each curry paste its distinct color depends on whether curry powder or chilies have been added to the mix. Yellow curry paste gets its color from curry powder, which contains tur-meric, and is the sweetest kind of curry paste. Green curry paste contains green chilies and has a brighter, sharper flavor than other curry pastes. Thick red curry paste gets its color and bold spiciness from red chilies. A sealed con-tainer of curry paste can last up to a month in the refrigerator. My favorite brands are Maesri and Mae Ploy.

Curry powder Curry powder is traditionally made from ground turmeric, coriander, cumin, and dried red pepper. Curry powder gives yel-low curry its distinct color and slightly sweet, tangy flavor. Curry powder's flavor "opens up" when heated, most often in coconut milk or oil. Curry powder is widely available in the spice section of your grocery store. American brands tend to run on the mild side, so go to an Asian or Indian market if you prefer a spicier curry powder.

Dark soy sauce Made from fermented soybeans, dark soy sauce is aged longer and is slightly sweeter and thicker than regular soy sauce. It sometimes contains molasses or caramel to deepen its color and thicken its consistency. Heating dark soy sauce releases its full, rich flavor in sauces and gravies used in stir-fries and noodle dishes like Pad Wee Ew and Thai Flat Noodles. It is also a popular ingredient in marinades and dipping sauces. Dark soy sauce can keep for a long time in a cool, dry place. Discontinue use if it has any crystallization around the opening of the bottle or shows any thickening at the bottom of the bottle. You can find dark soy sauce at Asian markets and some specialty stores.

Dried Thai Chilies

Thai Chilies

Chilies There are almost as many varieties of chilies as there are cultures. Thai chilies happen to be some of the hottest. Small or long, green or red, dried or fresh, Thai chilies are used in everything from curries and soups to sauces and flavored vinegar. The two most popular varieties are long Thai chili and small Thai chili. Small, bird or bird's-eye chili, is more common in the United States than long Thai chili, and ranges from mild to very hot. Wear rubber gloves when cutting hot chilies, or be sure to wash your hands thor-oughly afterwards to avoid getting the oil on your face or in your eyes. Also, wash cutting surfaces after chopping chilies or you may transfer the heat to other foods. I recommend using fresh jalapeño or Serrano chilies if you can't find Thai chilies. Deseed chilies if you prefer less heat or omit altogether or choose a milder type if cooking for young children.

Dried shrimp paste This pungent paste is made from fermented dried shrimp and salt and is used to make curry pastes, sauces, and soups. Sold in small jars or blocks, a little goes a long way! Dried shrimp paste should be used sparingly as it's quite pungent and strong in aroma. You'll only need this ingredient to make Roasted Red Chili Paste (page 23) in this book. Dried shrimp paste is available at Asian markets.

Fish sauce (nam pla) No Thai kitchen is complete without a bottle of fish sauce. In fact that goes for every kitchen throughout Southeast Asia. I collect bottles of fish sauce like other people collect bottles of wine. Fish sauces range from mild to strong and smoky to pungent. The finest ones are clear and light amber in color. Fish sauce is made from layering anchovies and salt in a sealed container for about six months then siphoning off the fermented liquid. Fish sauce's signature fishy, briny aroma dissipates when cooked. It emboldens and brings together the other flavors in any dish. I prefer ones with no sugar added so that the fishy aroma shines through. Fish sauce doesn't need to be refrigerated. It will keep indefinitely in the cupboard. As a general rule,

1 tablespoon of fish oil equals 1 teaspoon of salt. A good substitute is soy sauce mixed with a splash of oyster sauce or anchovy paste.

Five spice powder As the name suggests, this is a combination of five ground spices: star anise, Sichuan pepper, fennel, cloves and cinnamon. Complexly pungent and spicy with a hint of sweetness, it can be found in Asian markets and some grocery stores.

Galangal is similar to ginger, but galangal has a more lemony, piney taste and less pungent heat. Harder than ginger, with a thicker, tougher skin, galangal distinguishes itself by its lovely pink color. Rarely used on its own, galangal is a lovely complement to lemongrass, garlic, chili, and onions in curries, soups, and stir-fries. A wonderful meat tenderizer, galangal is also a popular ingredient in rubs and marinades. If you have trouble finding galangal, fresh ginger is a fine substitute.

Ginger is an incredibly popular ingredient in Thai and other Asian cuisines, fresh ginger has a spicy, sweet, peppery bite that is unmistakable. Heavy, firm pieces of fresh ginger are the best.

The most flavorful part of the root is the meat closest to the peel, so trim ginger with a light touch. The peel can be used to make a deliciously spicy and soothing tea. Powdered ginger is also available, but isn't as flavorful as fresh ginger.

Hoisin sauce is traditionally made from red rice brewed with soybean paste, garlic, sugar, star anise, chili paste, and other spices. It ranges in color from reddish brown to mahogany. It is a favorite marinade, glaze, and dipping sauce. Hoisin sauce has a very strong taste that can overpower other ingredients, so add it to a dish a little bit at a time until you get the flavor and heat you desire. Although nothing can truly match the flavor of hoisin sauce, Chinese barbecue sauce or tomato sauce blended with oyster sauce work can substitute in a pinch. Hoisin sauce is widely available at many grocery stores and Asian markets.

Jasmine rice is revered in Thailand as it is in other Asian countries so much so that is also referred to as "noble" rice or "beautiful" rice. Most Thai meals are accompanied by jasmine rice which is an aromatic, long-grain rice that

is tender and slightly sticky when cooked. Considered by many to be the most fragrant rice in the world, jasmine rice has a sweet, nutty aroma. Thailand produces the highest quality variety, but very good jasmine rice is also grown in Texas. Thai cooking mostly calls for white jasmine rice, but brown jasmine rice is available as well.

Kaffir lime leaves have a distinct hourglass shape, glossy shine, and a complex aroma that evokes orange, clove, lime, and citrus. Whole or sliced leaves are commonly used as a garnish or added to curries, stir-fries, soups, and salads. Kaffir lime leaves can also be crushed or ground to add a deliciously tangy and citrusy flavor to sauces. Dried kaffir lime leaves don't have much flavor, so a better substitute would be young, fresh lemon, lime, or grapefruit leaves. Kaffir lime leaves are not easy to find so I've made them optional for the recipes in this book.

Lemongrass has a delicious lemony woodsy flavor without the acidity or sharpness of an actual lemon. The most tender and edible parts of this thin, reedy plant are the bulb and lower 3–4 inches (7.5–10 cm) of the inner core.

Chopped, sliced or ground, fresh lemongrass is used in curry pastes and soups, and pairs especially well with galangal. Buy fresh lemongrass in bunches at Asian markets or at some farmers markets during the summer. Chopped fresh lemongrass freezes well, which comes in handy when a bowl of soothing lemongrass-scented soup is desired on a cold winter's night. A substitute for lemongrass is sliced lime leaves, or sliced lime or lemon rind. If fresh lemongrass isn't available you can use frozen lemongrass or minced lemongrass in a tube available in the produce section of some grocery stores.

Oyster sauce Brewed from dried oysters, salt and water, oyster sauce has a deep, rich brown color. The best varieties are thick and rich, with a distinct oyster aroma, which dissipates when cooked. Oyster sauce is slightly sweet and makes a less salty alternative to soy sauce. It is used as an ingredient in stir-fries, a table condiment, marinade, and barbecue sauce. A substitute for oyster is soy sauce blended with fish sauce.

Palm sugar Nicknamed the "maple sugar of the tropics," palm sugar is made by boiling down the sap of the coconut palm tree or sugar palm tree. It has a light caramel color and tastes a bit like maple syrup with a slightly smokier taste. It is commonly sold in a solid disc or block, but it is also available granulated or in a paste. Solid palm sugar should be grated, shaved, or melted before adding it to sweets, drinks, curries, and other dishes. Palm sugar is increasing in popularity throughout the U.S. If you can't get your hands on any, then dark brown sugar or maple syrup makes a good substitute.

Roasted red chili paste (nam prik pao) Roasted red chili paste is a blend of ground red pepper and other ingredients like garlic, shallots, dried shrimp paste, and tamarind. Intense and complex, it is packed with so much flavor that a little goes a long way. A staple of Thai cuisine, it is featured in soups, sauces, stir-fries, and rice dishes. It can also be enjoyed on its own as a lively dip or spread.

Sambal oelek is a fiery red chili-garlic paste used as a condiment and cooking ingredients all over Malaysia and Thailand. Traditionally, little more is added to the chilies than water, salt, garlic, or vinegar. Sambal oelek adds significant heat without overpowering the other flavors in a dish.

Sriracha sauce Traditional Sriracha sauce is a hot chili paste named after the seaside town where it originated. The most popular Sriracha sauce in the United States is Huy Fong Sriracha Hot Chili Sauce, affectionately known as "Rooster Sauce" because of the picture of the rooster on the bottle. Made from red jalapeño chilies, vinegar, garlic, sugar, and salt, it has a rich, complex flavor and significant heat. Many fans of Srircha don't limit it to Thai food—they put it on everything from eggs to pizza and more. Kikkoman also produces a Sriracha sauce available at grocery stores.

Dried Glass Noodles

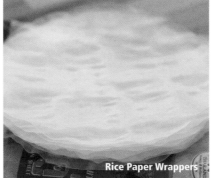
Rice Paper Wrappers

Flat Wide Rice Noodles

Rice Sticks

Rice Vermicelli Noodles

Dried glass noodles Also known as cellophane noodles, bean thread noodles, and Chinese vermicelli, these delicate thread noodles are made from green mung bean flour. Dried glass noodles are presoaked in hot water for a few minutes before cooking, unless they are added to a soup or deep-fried. Like tofu, bean thread noodles absorb the flavors of the other ingredients in a dish.

Rice noodles Thin or wide, flat or round, rice noodles come in many shapes and sizes. Made from rice flour and water, rice noodles are available dried or fresh. Dried rice noodles can be presoaked and softened in hot water before cooking, or they can be dropped directly into hot oil for crispy noodles—for a dramatic "explosive" effect. Packaged fresh noodles are usually coated with oil to prevent clumping, so you might want to give them a rinse before cooking.

Rice sticks come in a variety of widths. Thin sticks work well for soups and steamed noodle dishes. Wider rice sticks are ideal for stir-fries like the ever-popular pad Thai. Most commonly sold dry, rice sticks start out opaque and become transparent when soaked in water. Fresh rice sticks can be found in any Asian market.

Rice vermicelli noodles Also known as rice threads, vermicelli rice noodles are usually sold dried and in a block. The noodles should be presoaked when being used in spring rolls, stir-fries and salads. They can also be dropped straight from the package into soups or into hot oil to make crispy noodle dishes like mee krob.

Flat wide rice noodles Wider than rice sticks, these noodles are most famously used for Thai Flat Noodles (page 104) a popular stir-fry dish made with thick brown gravy, broccoli, and a protein like meat, seafood or tofu. Also known as river noodles, they hold up better in heavy gravy than thinner noodles. They're sold fresh or dried.

Rice paper wrappers Rice paper is made by mixing white rice flour and water, then spreading the mixture out into thin sheets and steaming them or sun-drying them. Rice paper serves as the wrap for spring rolls and other rollups like summer rolls. Before using rice paper it must be moistened in warm water or by carefully holding them over steam.

Sticky rice (sweet or glutinous rice) A beloved staple in Thai cuisine, sticky, sweet or glutinous rice is a medium to long grain variety of rice that becomes sticky when cooked. Traditionally steamed, not boiled, sticky rice is used in both sweet and savory dishes, and is usually eaten by hand in Thailand.

Tamarind is the pod-like fruit of the tamarind tree. There are two varieties of tamarind: tart and sour-sweet. Fresh tart tamarind is eaten with salt and chili, or chopped into chili paste. The pulp of tart tamarind is often added to soups, curries, sauces, and stir-fries. Sour-sweet tamarind is mostly used in making desserts and candy. Its flavor can be described as a cross between a date, sour-sweet guava, and an apricot. Tamarind concentrate or paste is available in jars, bottles, and solid blocks. Tamarind concentrate is mixed with water to create tamarind water. A substitute for tamarind concentrate or paste is date purée mixed with lime juice or combine equal parts vinegar, soy sauce, and sugar.

Turmeric found in most kitchens is the powdered form made from the turmeric root, which looks a lot like fresh ginger. Turmeric powder has a deep yellow color and a lovely rose aroma. It is used in curries, marinades, rice dishes, and when pickling. Turmeric powder is a powerful natural dye so handle it with care because it can permanently stain clothing. Prized in its own right, turmeric powder also makes an inexpensive alternative to saffron when combined with ground clove, cardamom, and cinnamon. Fresh turmeric is also available, but it can be a little bitter.

Spring roll wrappers can be found at Asian markets and come in 4-inch (10 cm) or 8-inch (20 cm) squares. They fry up light and crispy and are used for the Banana Spring Roll (page 138) in this book.

Star anise is the seedpod of a small tree found throughout Asia. The star-shaped spice has a warm, rich and pungent aroma of licorice, cinnamon, and clove. The actual seeds inside the pod are tiny, black and have no flavor. Used whole to add a subtle aroma or ground for maximum flavor, star anise is a popular ingredient in soups, curries, sweets and teas. A substitute for star anise is a blend of ground cloves and cinnamon.

Straw mushrooms get their name because they are cultivated on beds of straw. They are actually shaped like little helmets and have a delicate, sweet flavor. They are the most widely used mushroom in traditional Thai cooking and are added to soups, curries, stir-fries, and more. Fresh straw mushrooms can be hard to find in the United States, but the canned variety are available at most Asian markets.

Yard-long beans or **long bean**s Summertime brings an abundance of fresh long beans, or yard-long beans, to Asian markets. They get their name because they really can grow to be about a yard in length. Long beans look and taste a bit like regular green beans, but their taste, texture, and juiciness don't hold up as well when boiled or steamed. They really come alive when stir-fried or deep-fried. If you can't find yard-long beans, you can substitute with fresh green beans.

Yellow bean paste Also known as soy bean paste or yellow bean paste, yellow bean paste is made from fermented sweet yellow soybeans. Yellow bean paste adds a light, malty flavor to noodle dishes and curries. You'll only need this ingredient to make Thai Flat Noodles (page 104). I like the Healthy Boy brand with a drawing of an adorable little boy on the label.

The Basics

While traveling throughout Thailand you will notice that all of the restaurant tables are filled with various condiments from fish sauce to vinegar and chili sauce. You see, Thai people like to pour a "little of this here" and top with "a little of that there" until they've created their perfect balance of sweet, sour, hot, and salty, according to their palate and whim for the day. This is a collection of some basic sauces and condiments that can be used to enhance flavors while cooking or as a condiment such as Roasted Red Chili Paste (page 23) or popular dipping sauces like Sweet Thai Chili Sauce (page 24) and Hoisin Peanut Sauce (page 25). I've also included basic recipes which are the backbone of popular Thai recipes like Basic Curry Sauce (page 26) or Basic Chicken Stock (page 26). The variety of sauces and dips in Thai cuisine is far and wide so this is by no means a comprehensive collection. I believe what I offer here will give you the flexibility to "add little bit here" and "a little bit there" to satisfy your budding Thai palate as well as letting you improvise with the recipes in this book.

Ginger Lime Dipping Sauce

This refreshing dip is a fantastic accompaniment to the Chiang Mai Chicken in Lettuce Cups (page 34). It's the perfect balance of sweet, sour, and hot flavors. If you like a lot of heat, then skip the deseeding but watch your tongue!

MAKES 1 CUP (250 ML)
PREPARATION TIME: 5 MINUTES
COOKING TIME: 10 MINUTES

½ cup (125 ml) water
½ cup (100 g) sugar
1 tablespoon peeled and minced fresh ginger
4 tablespoons freshly squeezed lime juice
1 teaspoon rice vinegar or white vinegar
2 teaspoons fish sauce (nam pla)
1 fresh hot red or green pepper, preferably Thai, deseeded and finely sliced

Bring sugar and water to a boil in a saucepan, stirring to dissolve the sugar. Cool slightly. Mix ¼ cup (65 ml) of the syrup with the ginger, lime juice, vinegar, fish sauce, and chili in a small bowl. Transfer to a small serving bowl. Discard the remaining syrup.

COOK'S NOTE: If you can't find Thai chilies, I recommend using jalapeño or Serrano chilies.

Roasted Red Chili Paste (Nam Prik Pao)

Roasted Red Chili Paste, or Nam Prik Pao adds an amazing "je ne sais quoi" to stir-fry dishes, soups and anything that can use an added rich and complex kick in the pants. Once I started experimenting with this jam-like sauce, I couldn't seem to get enough of it and love having it on hand. It's my secret weapon for creating mouth-watering Thai dishes and will soon be yours too. Increase the amount of ground red pepper (cayenne) if you want extra heat. Fermented shrimp paste and tamarind concentrate can be found at most Asian markets.

MAKES 1 SMALL JAR
PREPARATION TIME: 5 MINUTES
COOKING TIME: 15 MINUTES

4 tablespoons high-heat cooking oil, divided
6 garlic cloves, minced
6 tablespoons finely chopped shallots
1 tablespoon ground red pepper (cayenne)
4 teaspoons fermented shrimp paste
2 tablespoons fish sauce (nam pla)
3 tablespoons palm or brown sugar
1 tablespoon freshly squeezed lime juice
1 teaspoon tamarind concentrate
1 tablespoon water

1 Heat the oil in a wok or skillet at medium high heat. Add the garlic and shallots and stir-fry until fragrant, about 30 seconds. Transfer garlic and shallots to a small bowl with a slotted spoon. Set aside. Leave the remaining oil in the pan.

2 Combine the ground red pepper, shrimp paste, fish sauce, brown sugar, lime juice, tamarind concentrate, water, reserved garlic, and shallots in a small food processor. Pulse until a thick paste forms.

3 Return the paste to the wok or skillet and stir it into the oil over low heat. Simmer gently and continue stirring until the mixture is a smooth, oily, and shimmering paste.

How to Make Roasted Red Chili Paste

1 Measure the sauce ingredients and place into individual bowls.

2 Heat the oil in a wok or skillet and add garlic and shallots.

3 Stir-fry the shallots and garlic until fragrant. Remove with a slotted spoon.

4 Combine the remaining sauce ingredients and reserved shallots and garlic in a small food processor.

5 Pulse in food processor until a thick paste forms.

Sweet Thai Chili Sauce

Oh, Sweet Thai Chili Sauce, how do I love thee? Let me count the ways. This versatile sauce is so easy to make yet adds so much tangy sweet flavor to everything it touches. Although it's perfectly okay to use the store-bought stuff, I try to make it from scratch because it's really so easy to make. Once you have it on hand you'll realize all the great uses for it, from drizzling on crab cakes to sweetening up a spicy stir-fry. The crushed red pepper also give it a gorgeous hue and is so pretty when wrapped up in a sterilized jar (hey, what an original hostess gift).

MAKES ¾ CUP (180 ML)
PREPARATION TIME: 5 MINUTES
COOKING TIME: 15 MINUTES

½ cup (125 ml) rice vinegar or white vinegar
4 tablespoons water
⅓ cup (67 g) sugar
3 garlic cloves, minced
½ teaspoon crushed red pepper
½ teaspoon salt
1 tablespoon all-purpose cornstarch mixed with 2 tablespoons water

Bring vinegar, water, sugar, garlic, crushed red pepper, and salt to a boil. Cook until the liquid is reduced by half, about 8 minutes. Reduce heat to low and add all-purpose cornstarch mixture. Stir until thickened, about 1 minute. Remove from heat and let cool completely.

COOK'S NOTE: Store the Sweet Thai Chili Sauce in a sealed glass jar in the refrigerator for up to several months.

Spicy Peanut Sauce

Satay is all about the sauce and this sauce is boss. I like to make homemade peanut butter when I have the time by simply blending roasted peanuts with a bit of honey and some peanut oil in the food processor, but store-bought peanut butter is completely fine. This is the perfect marriage of creamy nutty flavor with smooth coconut milk and just enough heat from the crushed red pepper. Great for any satay, especially for the Chicken Satay with Spicy Peanut Sauce (page 31), but also a yummy sauce for noodles or drizzled in a Thai wrap sandwich.

MAKES ½ CUP
PREPARATION TIME: 5 MINUTES
COOKING TIME: 8 MINUTES

3 tablespoons smooth peanut butter
4 tablespoons coconut milk
1 teaspoon thick red curry paste
1 tablespoon freshly squeezed lime juice
2 teaspoons soy sauce
2 teaspoons palm or brown sugar
½ teaspoon crushed red pepper
Crushed roasted peanuts for garnish

Heat the peanut butter, coconut milk, thick red curry paste, lime juice, soy sauce, brown sugar, and red pepper over medium-low heat in small saucepan until the mixture begins to simmer, stirring constantly. Transfer to a small serving bowl and garnish with peanuts.

COOK'S NOTE: Add a bit more coconut milk if you prefer a thinner sauce.

Sweet Hot Garlic Sauce

This is an incredibly simple, yet elegant sauce that can transform everyday grilled meats into glossy, lacquered treats. You can use chili-garlic sauce, sambal oelek, or crushed red pepper in place of the Sriracha if you'd like. This is another sauce that is wonderful to keep on hand to toss with stir-fried veggies or toss with some wings for a sticky sweet appetizer with some lovely heat.

MAKES ½ CUP (125 ML)
PREPARATION TIME: 5 MINUTES
COOKING TIME: 10 MINUTES

1 cup (200 g) sugar
6 cloves garlic, minced
½ cup (125 ml) water
½ teaspoon salt
½ cup (125 ml) rice vinegar or white vinegar
3–4 teaspoons Asian chili sauce, preferably Sriracha

Bring the sugar, garlic, water, salt, and vinegar to a boil in a saucepan stirring until sugar is dissolved. Reduce heat to low. Simmer until mixture thickens to a syrupy consistency. Remove from the heat and stir in the Sriracha. Transfer to a small serving bowl. Cool to room temperature before serving.

Hoisin Peanut Sauce

This sweet and nutty, yet tangy dip is killer! It's most commonly served with the herb-filled Summer Rolls with Shrimp and Mint (page 32). It's so simple to make and goes great with veggies and even pretzels. Add some chili sauce for an added kick experiment or with chunky peanut butter for a crunchier texture.

MAKES ¾ CUP (180 ML)
PREPARATION TIME: 5 MINUTES
COOKING TIME: 10 MINUTES

½ cup (125 ml) hoisin sauce
2 tablespoons creamy peanut butter
2 tablespoons water
1 tablespoon rice or white vinegar
Crushed roasted peanuts for garnish

Bring hoisin sauce, peanut butter, water, and vinegar to a boil in a saucepan over moderately-high heat. Immediately remove from heat. Transfer to a small serving bowl. Garnish sauce with crushed peanuts.

Basic Curry Sauce

In a hurry, but craving curry? Then this basic sauce is for you. Throw in some leftover roast chicken or a handful of tofu and veggies while it's simmering for an easy peasy, soul satisfying meal. Smash a Thai chili and add to the sauce with the coconut milk to raise the heat-o-meter.

MAKES 1¾ CUPS (430 ML) CURRY SAUCE
PREPARATION TIME: 5 MINUTES
COOKING TIME: 15 MINUTES

1 tablespoon cooking oil
1 garlic clove, minced
½ small white onion, finely chopped
1 tablespoon thick red curry paste
1 cup (250 ml) thick coconut milk
½ cup (125 ml) Basic Chicken Stock (page 26) or store-bought
1 tablespoon fish sauce (nam pla)
1 teaspoon palm or brown sugar

Heat the oil in a wok or deep skillet over medium-high heat. Add the garlic and onion and stir-fry until the garlic is fragrant and the onion is translucent, about 1 minute. Reduce heat to medium. Add the curry paste, stirring to break up paste, about 1 minute. Add the coconut milk, chicken broth, fish sauce, and palm sugar. Bring to a boil. Reduce heat to medium-low, cover and simmer for 10–12 minutes.

Cilantro Lime Soy Sauce

This is a bright sauce filled with flavor that I love to serve with dumplings and even shrimp cocktail. It's also a light and delightful marinade for chicken or fish. I also make a quick veggie tofu stir-fry dish using this sauce whenever my vegan friend Kelly comes over and she always asks for seconds.

MAKES 1 CUP (250 ML)
PREPARATION TIME: 10 MINUTES

1 teaspoon finely chopped shallots
1 fresh hot red or green chili, preferably Thai (deseeded if you prefer less heat), finely sliced
2 tablespoons minced lemongrass
4 tablespoons fresh coriander leaves (cilantro)
4 tablespoons soy sauce
2 tablespoons freshly squeezed lime juice
3 tablespoons water
2 tablespoons sugar

Combine all of the ingredients in a small food processor or blender until blended. Transfer to a small serving bowl

Basic Chicken Stock

My late mother always taught me that a good homemade broth is the backbone of Asian cooking. I try to make this in large batches and freeze it so I always have it on hand. The key is boiling the chicken bones briefly first, rinsing and returning them to the pot. The results are clean and superior, enough to make any mother proud.

MAKES 2 QUARTS (1.75 LITERS)
PREPARATION TIME: 5 MINUTES
COOKING TIME: 2½ HOURS + COOLING TIME

2½ lbs (1.25 kg) boney chicken pieces
Three ¼ in (6 mm) slices peeled fresh galangal or ginger
4 garlic cloves, smashed
2 stalks lemongrass, use the bottom 6 in (15 cm) of the stalk with outer leaves removed, smash with knife
2 quarts (1.75 liters) water
4 oz (100 g) coarsely chopped fresh coriander stems (cilantro)

Fill a stock pot ⅔ full with water and bring a boil. Add chicken bones and boil for 3 minutes. Pour out the water and rinse the bones. Return the bones to the stock pot. Add the galangal, garlic, lemongrass, and the water. Cover and bring to a boil. Reduce the heat to medium low. Skim the fat and foam off the top. Add the fresh coriander stems (cilantro). Simmer uncovered for 2 hours, continue to skim the foam off the top frequently. Strain and cool before storing in refrigerator.

Basic Fish Stock

Fish stock requires a lot less time to simmer than chicken stock. Stir-frying the bones briefly eliminates the fishy smell and flavor from this stock which is key to creating clean and bright tasting seafood soups and sauces.

MAKES 2 QUARTS (1.75 LITERS)
PREPARATION TIME: 5 MINUTES
COOKING TIME: 50 MINUTES + COOLING TIME

1 tablespoon oil
1 lb (500 g) fish bones with heads (gills removed)
Three ¼ in (6mm) thick galangal or fresh ginger slices
4 garlic cloves, smashed
2 stalks lemongrass, bottom 6 in (15 cm) only with outer leaves removed and smashed
2 oz (50 g) coarsely chopped fresh coriander stems (cilantro)
2 quarts (1.75 liters) water

Heat the oil in a stock pot over moderately high-heat. Add the fish bones and stir-fry for about 3 minutes, or until pink. Add the galangal, garlic, lemongrass, and 2 quarts (1.75 liters) water. Cover and bring to a boil. Reduce the heat to medium-low and simmer uncovered for 15 minutes. Skim the fat and foam off the top. Add the fresh coriander stems. Simmer uncovered for 20 minutes, continuing to skim the foam off the top often. Strain and cool before storing in refrigerator.

A Side of Spicy Thai Cukes

I could munch on this cucumber condiment morning, noon and night. Thai people love to serve a side of cukes to add a crunch and spicy, yet cooling, accompaniment to everything from a savory curry to satay. It's also excellent with fried rice and spring rolls.

MAKES 2½ CUPS (260 G)
PREPARATION TIME: 10 MINUTES

2 cucumbers, peeled, seeded, and diced
2 small shallots, thinly sliced
2 tablespoons finely chopped fresh coriander leaves (cilantro)
1 teaspoon finely sliced fresh hot red or green chili, preferably Thai (deseeded if you prefer less heat)
1 tablespoon crushed roasted peanuts for garnish

DRESSING
1 garlic clove, minced
4 tablespoons rice or white vinegar
4 tablespoons sugar
¼ teaspoon salt
2 tablespoons water

1 In a small bowl whisk together the ingredients for the Dressing.
2 Combine the cucumber, shallots, fresh coriander leaves, and chili in a medium bowl and toss to combine with the dressing. Garnish with the peanuts.

CHAPTER ONE

Appetizers and Snacks

Thai people love to snack. It seems that Thai people are constantly enjoying a meal or snacking. They love snacking so much that you will find street vendors and bustling market stalls at all hours of the day and night filled with a dizzying array of Thai favorites from satays to spring rolls and dried insects!

While I'm not a fan of dried bugs, I absolutely love Thai appetizers and snacks. I've created a collection here that you can make easily for a party just for your family.

The Lemongrass Chicken Wings (page 30) are a huge hit during the Super Bowl at our house and the Panaeng Curry Meatballs (page 39) are mild and flavorful and great for potlucks. The Chiang Mai Chicken in Lettuce Cups (page 34) are tender and flavorful and the dipping sauce is bright and fresh. For seafood lovers, the Steamed Mussels with Lemongrass and Basil (page 35) are bursting with flavor, super easy and so healthy. The Thai Crab Cakes (page 36) have just the right crunch and the dipping sauces are killer. We've become officially addicted to the Sweet and Spicy Thai Glazed Cashews (page 39), which are fantastic on salads and ice cream or to munch while enjoying a Thai beer.

I think you'll find that there's something for everyone in this chapter.

If you're cooking for a party you can simply double or triple the recipe. As with most Thai recipes, you can do the prep in advance and do the cooking just as your friends pop by. I like to make extra batches of Black Pepper Garlic Spare Ribs (page 38) and freeze them for when unexpected guests arrive. I defrost them in the microwave and throw them in the oven to reheat. I think you'll enjoy these appetizers and snacks as much as my friends and family do. Happy snacking!

Lemongrass Chicken Wings

These sweet, sour, and salty wings are sure to be a hit with your family and friends. Double or triple the recipe for your next Super Bowl gathering and add an Asian twist to the festivities.

SERVES 4–6 AS AN APPETIZER OR SNACK
PREPARATION TIME: 10 MINUTES + MARINATING TIME
COOKING TIME: 25 MINUTES

1½ lbs (750 g) chicken wings
2 tablespoons crushed roasted peanuts
2 tablespoons finely chopped fresh coriander leaves (cilantro)

MARINADE
2 cloves garlic, minced
2 tablespoons finely chopped shallots
2 teaspoons minced galangal or fresh ginger
2 tablespoons minced lemongrass
1 tablespoon palm or brown sugar
3 tablespoons fish sauce (nam pla)
1½ tablespoons freshly squeezed lime juice
2 tablespoons oil

1 Whisk together the Marinade ingredients in a large mixing bowl. Place chicken wings in a large resealable food storage bag. Pour the Marinade mixture over the chicken wings. Refrigerate for 2–12 hours.
2 Pre-heat a broiler. Arrange the wings on a broiler pan, top down. Broil the wings for 10–11 minutes, turn over and broil for another 10–11 minutes until golden brown, remove from the broiler and garnish with peanuts and fresh coriander leaves. Serve immediately.

Sweet & Spicy Thai Glazed Cashews

These sweet and spicy cashews are so addicting that one time I had to lock them in a cabinet so my husband wouldn't devour them all. The honey creates a glorious glaze punctuated with sweet, salty, and hot notes. They're a fantastic snack with Thai beer or Lemongrass Ginger Ale (page 136) and are also excellent in salads or sprinkled on top of Coconut Thai Basil Ice Cream (page 134).

SERVES 6 AS A SNACK
PREPARATION TIME: 5 MINUTES
COOKING TIME: 10–15 MINUTES + COOLING TIME

¼ cup (85 g) honey
1 tablespoon curry powder
1 teaspoon red pepper powder (cayenne)
2 teaspoons oil
1 teaspoon fish sauce (nam pla)
4 cups (140 g) cashews

1 Combine the honey, curry powder, red pepper powder, oil, and fish sauce in a medium bowl. Add the cashews and stir to combine.
2 Preheat the oven to 300°F (150°C). Spread the cashews in a single layer on a sheet pan. Bake for 10–15 minutes, turning often with a wide spatula, until golden brown. Remove from the oven and continue turning as they cool. Serve warm or at room temperature.

COOK'S NOTE: For a tropical twist, add ¼ cup (18 g) shredded coconut before baking.

Chicken Satay with Spicy Peanut Sauce

I remember enjoying chicken satay strolling through a night market in Bangkok. This delicious and simple appetizer is great to make ahead of time because it can marinate overnight and then cooks in just 3–5 minutes. I like to make the sauce in advance too. When I get home, I usually have my stepdaughter Kyla help skewer the chicken and we're enjoying this yummy snack within minutes. The simple marinade is flavorful yet not overpowering and the Spicy Peanut Sauce (page 24) is a match made in heaven. You may substitute the chicken with pork or beef if you wish.

SERVES 4–6 AS AN APPETIZER OR SNACK
PREPARATION TIME: 10 MINUTES +
MARINATING TIME
COOKING TIME: 20 MINUTES

1 lb (500 g) skinless, boneless chicken
  breasts or chicken thigh, cut into 1
  in (2.5 cm) strips
14 wooden skewers, soaked in water
  for 30 minutes
Oil, for grilling
Butter lettuce leaves
Fresh coriander leaves (cilantro)
½ cup (125 ml) Spicy Peanut Sauce
  (page 24)

YOGURT MARINADE
½ teaspoon salt
1 cup (250 g) plain yogurt
1 teaspoon minced galangal or fresh
  ginger
1 clove garlic, minced
1 tablespoon curry powder

1 Yogurt Marinade: Combine the salt, yogurt, galangal, garlic, and curry powder in a medium bowl, stir to combine. Place the chicken strips in the Yogurt Marinade and gently toss until well coated. Cover and refrigerate for at least 30 minutes (up to overnight).
2 Thread the chicken pieces onto the soaked skewers. Heat a grill pan over medium heat and brush it with oil. Grill the skewers 3–5 minutes on each side, until nicely seared. Serve immediately with lettuce leaves, fresh coriander leaves, and Spicy Peanut Sauce, allowing guests to remove the wooden skewer and enjoy the chicken wrapped in a lettuce leaf.

Summer Rolls with Shrimp and Mint

These delicate herb-filled rolls are so delicious and healthy. They're great to have at parties because your friends can get into the act and make their own rolls (omit the shrimp for vegetarians). They may be called Summer Rolls but you'll want to enjoy them all year round. Rolls can be made several hours in advance and stored at room temperature in an airtight container lined with dampened paper towels.

I love to serve these rolls with a spicy soup like Tom Yum Gai for a fun girl's lunch: high in flavor, but low in fat. The Hoisin Peanut Sauce (page 25) is divine and you'll want to double the recipe just to keep some on hand.

SERVES 8 AS AN APPETIZER OR SNACK

PREPARATION TIME: 45 MINUTES

2 oz (50 g) dried rice vermicelli
1 teaspoon salt
1 teaspoon dark sesame oil
16 medium-sized raw shrimp
1 package 12 in (30 cm) round rice paper wrappers
1 cup (100 g) fresh bean sprouts, ends trimmed
1 cup (105 g) carrots cut into matchsticks
4 tablespoons fresh mint leaves
4 tablespoons fresh basil leaves
8 large or 16 small red-leaf lettuce leaves, cut in half lengthwise
4 tablespoons crushed roasted peanuts
4 tablespoons Hoisin Peanut Sauce (page 25)

1 Place the rice vermicelli in a large bowl. Pour enough hot water over them to cover. Let stand until softened, about 10 minutes. Drain and rinse with cool water. Toss with 1 teaspoon of sesame oil.

2 Add the shrimp to boiling water; reduce heat to medium. Cook shrimp until it turns pink, about 2–3 minutes. Drain. When cool, remove the shells. Cut each shrimp in half lengthwise, devein, and set aside.

3 Fill a large, flat bowl with warm water, making sure it is large enough to fit the rice paper wrappers. Lay a clean towel on the workspace in front of you. Carefully dip a round wrapper into the water, just to get it wet all over, trying not to crack it. It will still be slightly hard. Remove it from the water and lay it onto the clean towel, where it will continue to soften.

4 Layer a small amount of each of the ingredients on the bottom ⅓ of the wrap. Start with a lettuce leaf, then about 1 tablespoon of bean sprouts, then 2–3 pieces of shrimp, then some noodles, followed by some shreds of carrot, and then top with 2 leaves of basil and 2 leaves of mint. Fold up the bottom ⅓, fold in the sides and roll up the rest of the length to make an egg roll shape. Set aside and continue with the rest of the ingredients until all of the rice wrappers are used.

5 Cut rolls in half on a diagonal. Serve with Hoisin Peanut Sauce for dipping.

COOK'S NOTE: Make sure to use warm, not hot water, when soaking rice paper wrappers. I used to soak them bit too long and they'd fall apart. After lots of practice, I realized that the wrappers should still be slightly stiff so don't over soak!

How to Assemble the Summer Rolls

1 After the shrimp is cooked, remove shells and cut each shrimp in half lengthwise and devein.

4 Fold in the left and right sides of the wrapper.

2 Measure the summer roll ingredients in individual bowls and place with the shrimp in preparation for rolling.

5 Close off the ends as if making an envelope.

3 Layer a small amount of each of the ingredients on the bottom 1/3 of the wrap. Fold up the bottom 1/3 tightly.

6 Continue rolling all the way to the top and press the seam closed to resemble an eggroll.

Chiang Mai Chicken in Lettuce Cups

This dish is inspired by the quintessential Northern Thai dish, Laab or Larb with Laotian origins. It's a simple dish made with minced meat and is bursting with flavor. My husband and I enjoyed many varieties as we zipped around Chiang Mai on a motorbike. We rewarded ourselves with this tasty treat every time we survived another harrowing journey on the Mae Hong Son pass.

This tasty snack is quick and easy to make, my friend Kristin loved it so much after having it at a dinner party at my house she stopped at the market on the way home to make it for lunch the next day. The tender chicken with the crunchy water chestnuts creates a wonderful texture. Substitute ground turkey for the chicken if you wish.

SERVES 4 AS AN APPETIZER OR SNACK
PREPARATION TIME: 10 MINUTES
COOKING TIME: 6 MINUTES

2 tablespoons oil
2 teaspoons minced galangal or fresh ginger
1 clove garlic, minced
1 fresh red or green chili, preferably Thai, finely sliced (deseeded if you prefer less heat)
½ lb (250 g) ground chicken

½ cup (75 g) canned chopped water chestnuts, rinsed and drained
1 tablespoon finely chopped fresh coriander leaves (cilantro)
1 tablespoon finely chopped green onion (scallion), white and green parts
1 tablespoon minced lemongrass
1 tablespoon fish sauce (nam pla)
1 teaspoon crushed red pepper
Salt and freshly ground black pepper
8 large butter lettuce leaves
Ginger Lime Dipping Sauce (page 22)

1 Heat oil in a wok or skillet on moderately-high heat. Add galangal, garlic, and chili and stir-fry until fragrant, about 30 seconds. Add ground chicken and stir-fry for 4 minutes. Add water chestnuts and stir-fry for 2 minutes.
2 Add fresh coriander leaves, green onion, lemongrass, fish sauce, crushed red pepper, and stir-fry for 30 seconds. Season with salt and pepper. Transfer to a serving bowl.
3 Serve chicken mixture with lettuce leaves and Ginger Lime Dipping Sauce, allowing guests to form their own wraps.

Steamed Mussels in Lemongrass and Basil

These soul-satisfying mussels are bursting with bright flavors and always fill my kitchen with an amazing aroma. Serve with a crusty French baguette to help soak up the juices. A white Riesling or blush wine pairs nicely with this dish.

SERVES 4 AS AN APPETIZER OR SNACK
PREPARATION TIME: 10 MINUTES + MUSSEL CLEANING TIME
COOKING TIME: 12 MINUTES

½ cup (125 ml) Basic Chicken Stock (page 26) or store-bought
2 tablespoons minced lemongrass
6 kaffir lime leaves, torn or cut in half (optional)
½ cup (125 ml) dry white wine
1 fresh hot red or green chili, preferably Thai, thinly sliced (deseeded if your prefer less heat)
2 tablespoons fish sauce (nam pla)
1 tablespoon palm or brown sugar
Two small handfuls of fresh coriander leaves (cilantro) (about ½ cup/24 g), finely chopped
1 lb (500 g) fresh mussels, debearded and scrubbed clean
1 clove garlic, minced
2 teaspoons all-purpose cornstarch dissolved in 1 tablespoon water
Fresh basil leaves for garnish
Fresh coriander leaves (cilantro) for garnish
Lime wedges

1 Pour the chicken stock into a wok or large skillet. Add the lemongrass and kaffir lime leaves, if using. Bring to a boil over high heat, then reduce to moderately-high.
2 Add the wine, chili slices, fish sauce, palm sugar, and fresh coriander leaves. Stir to combine. When the sauce is gently boiling, add the mussels. Stir to combine and cover with a tight-fitting lid. Cook for 2–3 minutes.
3 Remove the lid and gently stir the mussels. If some of them still haven't opened, put the lid back on and cook 1 more minute.
4 Reduce heat to low and add the garlic and stir gently. Push the mussels to the side of the pan. Add the all-purpose cornstarch mixture to the liquid in the pan, stirring until thickened. Once thickened, stir to combine.
5 Remove from heat. Scoop or slide the mussels into a large serving bowl (or individual bowls). Pour the remaining sauce on top. Garnish with basil and fresh coriander leaves. Serve immediately with lime wedges on the side.

COOK'S NOTE: It's best to purchase mussels right before cooking but if bought in advance keep moist on ice in the refrigerator. Just before cooking, scrub them with a stiff brush under cool running water and trim off beards if they have them. If any are open, tap the shell. If they don't close tightly, discard them. If they don't open when cooked also discard them.

Thai Crab Cakes

This recipe is inspired by the crab cakes my husband and I enjoyed during our honeymoon in southern Thailand while we were island hopping. I love to use fresh crab meat, but canned is fine too. I recommend serving these crunchy crab cakes with a Sriracha Mayo for creamy heat along with Sweet Thai Chili Sauce (page 24) for a contrasting taste sensation.

SERVES 4–6 AS AN APPETIZER OR SNACK
PREPARATION TIME: 30 MINUTES
COOKING TIME: 10 MINUTES

6 shelled and deveined medium-sized raw shrimp
1 teaspoon fish sauce (nam pla)
1 lb (500 g) lump crab meat, picked over for shells
3 large eggs, divided
3 tablespoons + 1 cup (65 g) panko bread crumbs, divided
4 tablespoons finely chopped green onions (white and green parts)
4 tablespoons finely chopped fresh coriander leaves (cilantro)
1 tablespoon freshly squeezed lime juice
1 fresh hot red or green chili, preferably Thai, finely minced (deseeded if you prefer less heat)
1 teaspoon minced galangal or fresh ginger
1 teaspoon salt
¼ teaspoon freshly ground black pepper
Vegetable oil for pan-frying
¾ cup (184 ml) homemade Sweet Thai Chili Sauce (page 24) or store-bought
Sriracha Mayo (recipe on right)
Lime wedges for serving

1 Purée the shrimp in a food processor until a smooth paste forms. Add the fish sauce and purée for 30 additional seconds. In a medium bowl, combine the shrimp purée, crab meat, egg, 3 tablespoons of bread crumbs, green onion, fresh coriander leaves, lime juice, chili, galangal, and salt and pepper. Place the mixture in the refrigerator until you are ready to cook so the patties will be easier to shape.

2 Shape crab meat mixture into 2¼ inches (5.5 cm) across and ¾ inches (2 cm) thick patties. Lightly beat the remaining two eggs in a bowl. Place 1 cup panko bread crumbs in a deep plate. Dip the patties one at a time in the egg mixture and then in the panko mixture until evenly coated.

3 Heat the oil in a large non-stick skillet on medium high heat. Working in batches, place the crab cakes in the pan (do not crowd the pan), and cook until golden brown, about 4 minutes on each side. Serve with Sweet Thai Chili Sauce, Sriracha Mayo and lime wedges.

COOK'S NOTE: I like to double this crab cake recipe and freeze a batch, then just thaw and reheat in a frying pan.

Sriracha Mayo

MAKES ½ CUP (125 G)

½ cup (125 g) mayonnaise
1 tablespoon Sriracha chili sauce
½ teaspoon freshly squeezed lime juice

Combine the mayonnaise, Srircha chili sauce, and lime juice until well blended.

How to Make the Crab Cakes

1 Measure the crab cake ingredients and place into individual bowls.

4 Shape the crab mixture into 2¼-inch (5.5 cm) and ¾-inch (2 cm) thick patties.

2 Mix the shrimp purée with the remaining crab cake ingredients in a medium bowl.

5 Dip the patties one at a time into the egg mixture and then into the panko bread crumbs until evenly coated.

3 Using a rubber spatula, place a small amount of the crab cake mixture in the palm of your hand.

6 Place the patties on a tray next to your stove top in preparation for frying.

Black Pepper Garlic Spare Ribs

These tasty riblets are satisfying and simple to make. Intense garlic and black pepper meet aromatic galangal and refreshing coriander leaves for a chorus of flavors that can't be beat. I love to serve these hearty ribs with Thai beer, a terrific complement to the ribs' peppery richness.

SERVES 4–6 AS AN APPETIZER OR SNACK
PREPARATION TIME: 15 MINUTES
COOKING TIME: 1½ HOURS

½ cup (50 g) finely sliced shallots
5 green onions, finely chopped (green and white parts)
One 2 in (5 cm) piece galangal, peeled and sliced into thin pieces
5 garlic cloves, smashed
Two small handfuls of fresh coriander leaves (cilantro) (about ½ cup/24 g), finely chopped
3 tablespoons soy sauce
1 tablespoon fish sauce (nam pla)
½ teaspoon salt
½ teaspoon freshly ground black pepper
1 tablespoon sugar
2 lbs (1 kg) pork rib tips, cut across the bone into 2–3 in (5–7.5 cm) sections

1 Put the shallots, green onions, galangal, garlic, fresh coriander leaves, soy sauce, fish sauce, salt, pepper, and sugar in the bowl of a food processor. Process into a loose, finely chopped paste, scraping down the sides of the bowl once or twice.
2 Place the pork tips in a large bowl, massaging the paste into the flesh for a minute or so. Cover and refrigerate for 5 hours (up to overnight). Toss the ribs occasionally while marinating.
3 Preheat oven to 350°F (175°C). Spread the ribs out, bone side down, on a parchment-lined sheet pan. Bake for 1½ hours. Remove from the oven and serve immediately.

Panaeng Curry Meatballs

This is a great dish to bring for potluck because it travels well and you can keep it warm for several hours. It usually draws lots of ooohs and ahhhhhs when I walk into a friend's house as the dish fills the room with exotic aromas from the galangal, curry, and fish sauce.

Panaeng curry is milder than other Thai curries so it's great for kids and adults alike. You can use thick red curry paste if you don't have Panaeng curry paste on hand.

SERVES 6 AS AN APPETIZER OR SNACK
PREPARATION TIME: 20 MINUTES
COOKING TIME: 25 MINUTES

1 lb (500 g) ground turkey
1 teaspoon minced galangal or fresh ginger
1 large egg
½ teaspoon salt
1 tablespoon high-heat cooking oil
1½ cups (375 ml) coconut milk
2 tablespoons Panaeng curry paste or thick red curry paste
½ cup (125 ml) water
1 tablespoon fish sauce (nam pla)
1 tablespoon palm or brown sugar
4–6 kaffir lime leaves (optional), torn in half
¼ cup (37 g) canned sliced bamboo shoots, rinsed and drained
Two small handfuls of fresh coriander leaves (cilantro) (about ½ cup/24 g), finely chopped

COOK'S NOTE: Try substituting turkey with ground pork or beef. For a spicier version of this dish, add ½ teaspoon of crushed red pepper to the turkey meat before forming into balls.

1 Mix the ground turkey with galangal, egg, and salt. Place approximately 1 teaspoon of the mixture and shape it into a meatball. Continue shaping and transfer them onto a platter.
2 Heat the oil in a skillet over medium-high heat. Add the meatballs and brown on all sides, about 5 minutes. Transfer to a plate and set aside.
3 Add the coconut milk to the frying pan and let it come a gentle simmer over medium heat for 5 minutes. Add the curry paste to the pan and cook about 3 minutes, stirring to dissolve the paste into the coconut milk. Return the meatballs and cook, turning gently to coat, 1–2 minutes.
4 Increase the heat to medium-high, bring to a gentle boil, and add the water, fish sauce, palm sugar, kaffir lime leaves (if using) and bamboo shoots. Reduce heat to low and simmer, stirring gently until the meatballs are cooked through, about 3–4 minutes. Remove from the heat, transfer to a serving bowl, and garnish with chopped fresh coriander leaves. Serve immediately.

Panaeng Curry Meatballs

How to Make the Panaeng Curry Meatballs

1 Combine the ground turkey, galangal, egg, and salt in a medium bowl.

2 Place about 1 teaspoon of the mixture in your hand and shape it into a meatball. Continue shaping the mixture into meatballs.

3 Brown the meatballs on all sides in a skillet over medium high heat for about 5 minutes.

4 Simmer coconut milk for 5 minutes and then add the curry paste and cook for 3 minutes.

5 Return the meatballs to the skillet and bring to a gentle boil. Add the water, fish sauce, palm sugar, kaffir lime leaves and bamboo shoots; simmer.

How to Make the Spring Rolls

1 After dipping the rice paper wrapper in warm water, carefully remove it onto a clean towel.

4 Continue rolling all the way to the top and press the seam closed to resemble an eggroll.

2 Spread 1 tablespoon of filling on the lower edge of the rice paper, near you, leaving a 1-inch (2.5 cm) edge.

5 Lay the finished spring rolls on a tray near your stove top in preparation for frying.

3 Fold the spring roll like an envelope by first folding over the lower 1-inch (2.5 cm) edge over the filling. Fold in the left and right sides of the wrapper.

6 Heat the oil to 350°F (175°C) and fry the rolls a few at a time until crisp, 6–8 minutes.

Crunchy Siam Spring Rolls

Thais love to snack. In Thailand, often only one main meal is eaten each day, the rest of the day is filled with small snacks from different street vendors. These crunchy spring rolls are a Thai street food favorite and are sure to become a favorite of your family's as well.

SERVES 4 AS AN APPETIZER OR SNACK
PREPARATION TIME: 40 MINUTES
COOKING TIME: 6–8 MINUTES

1 oz (25 g) dried glass noodles
4 dried black mushrooms
½ lb (250 g) pork
2 tablespoons finely chopped yellow onion
1 garlic clove, minced
1 small carrot, finely grated
1 egg, lightly beaten
½ tablespoon fish sauce (nam pla)
½ teaspoon salt
½ teaspoon freshly ground black pepper
Eight 8½ in (21.5 cm) round rice paper wrappers
Oil for frying
¾ cup (185 ml) homemade Sweet Thai Chili Sauce (page 24) or store-bought for dipping

COOK'S NOTE: The oil is ready for frying when a 1-inch (2.5 cm) cube of white bread dropped into the oil browns in 60 seconds.

1 Bring a saucepan of water to a boil. Remove from the heat. Immerse the noodles in hot water; let stand for 3–5 minutes stirring occasionally. Soak until noodles are soft, yet firm. Drain well and rinse. Cut the noodles into 1 inch (2.5 cm) lengths.

2 Soak the mushrooms in a medium bowl of hot water for 30 minutes. Drain and squeeze the water from the mushrooms thoroughly. Remove the stems and finely chop the mushrooms.

3 In a large bowl, combine the reserved noodles, reserved mushrooms, pork, onions, garlic, carrot, egg, fish sauce, salt, and pepper.

4 Fill a large, flat bowl with warm water, making sure it is large enough to fit the rice paper wrappers. Lay a clean towel on the workspace in front of you. Carefully dip the round wrapper into the water, just to get it wet all over, trying not to crack it. It will still be slightly hard Remove it from the water and lay it onto the clean towel, where it will continue to soften.

5 Spread 1 tablespoon of filling on the lower edge of the rice paper, near you, leaving a 1-inch (2.5 cm) edge. Begin to fold the spring roll like an envelope: first, fold over the lower 1 inch (2.5 cm) edge over the filing, then the left edge, then the right edge. Now roll the spring roll up to the top edge. Continue rolling until the filling is used.

6 In a large wok or deep skillet, heat 2–3 inches (5–7.5 cm) of the oil to 350°F (175°C). Fry the rolls a few at a time, turning occasionally, until crisp, 6–8 minutes. Drain on paper towels and serve with Sweet Thai Chili Sauce.

CHAPTER TWO

Soups

Unlike making soups in the U.S., Thai soups take very little time. Once you have your ingredients prepped, some Thai soups cook in just 15 minutes! The first time I made Thai soup, it was so quick I ended up waiting for my rice to finish steaming.

In Thailand, soups are usually served to complement multiple dishes where they are often sipped throughout the meal. Not only are Thai soups quick and easy, they're also bursting with fresh flavors from aromatic herbs, chilies, fresh lime juice, lemongrass, and spices.

Thai soups also happen to be very nourishing. In fact, many studies have been done on the cold and flu-busting potential of such Thai soups as Chicken Coconut Soup (page 51), the classic hot and sour chicken soup loaded with purported anti-oxidant properties.

Sour Spicy Shrimp Soup (page 50) is another one of my favorites, especially in the fall and winter months with its perfect balance of hot, sweet, sour and salty flavors. Tangy Pumpkin Soup (page 49) is a rustic treat, layered with spices and coconut milk that's both savory and sweet. Sizzling Rice Seafood Soup (page 47) is an homage to my Chinese roots, which takes a bit more time but is worth the extra effort. You'll see what I mean when the delicate, homemade rice crackers hit the soup with their signature sizzle.

Whether you're planning to serve Thai soup as part of a multi-course Thai meal or as a starter to some Italian pasta or as a simple lunch with a green salad, I think you will soon add these recipes to your soup repertoire.

Here's a time-saving tip: Spend a weekend afternoon making a large batch of homemade chicken stock (page 26) and freeze it so you'll always have it on hand to make great tasting Thai soups in a snap.

Shrimp Coconut Soup
(Tom Kah Goong)

I love to make this Thai comfort food on a chilly day when I want something light yet bursting with layered flavors. If you're able to find galangal, you'll notice a distinct earthy and mellow note compared to sharp and peppery ginger. I like to make the soup in advance and then throw in the shrimp just as my family arrives home as the shrimp cooks in just 4–5 minutes.

SERVES 4 AS PART OF A MULTI-COURSE MEAL
PREPARATION TIME: 10 MINUTES
COOKING TIME: 15 MINUTES

2 cups (500 ml) Basic Chicken Stock (page 26)
  or store-bought
Six ¼ in (6 mm) thick slices galangal or fresh ginger
2 stalks lemongrass, cut into 2 in (5 cm) long pieces and
  bruised
4 kaffir lime leaves, torn in half (optional)
1 tablespoon palm or brown sugar
1½ teaspoons Roasted Red Chili Paste (page 23) or store-
  bought, (nam prik pao, optional)
1 cup (250 ml) coconut milk
1 cup (70 g) sliced white button mushrooms
3 tablespoons freshly squeezed lime juice
2 tablespoons fish sauce (nam pla)
8 shelled and deveined medium-sized raw shrimp
2–3 fresh hot red or green chilies, preferably Thai,
  smashed
Fresh coriander leaves (cilantro) for garnish

1 Put the chicken stock, galangal, lemongrass, kaffir lime leaves (if using) palm sugar, and Roasted Red Chili Paste (if using) in a medium saucepan and bring to a boil over medium heat.
2 Add the coconut milk and mushrooms, reduce the heat and bring to a simmer. Simmer for 5 minutes.
3 Quickly stir in the lime juice and fish sauce. Remove from the heat and add the shrimp. Let stand for 4–5 minutes until the shrimp is cooked through. Float the chilies on the soup. Dish out into individual serving bowls and sprinkle with fresh coriander leaves. Serve immediately.

Chicken Coconut Soup
(Tom Kah Gai)

This cousin of Hot and Sour Chicken Soup (page 51), features coconut milk for a creamy and divine blend of sweet, hot, sour, and sweet flavors and is surprisingly simple to make. It's one of my favorite Thai soups and studies have shown that it may boost the immune system and ward off colds and the flu.

SERVES 4 AS PART OF A MULTI-COURSE MEAL
PREPARATION TIME: 10 MINUTES
COOKING TIME: 15 MINUTES

2 cups (500 ml) Basic Chicken Stock (see page 26) or store-bought
Six ¼ in (6 mm) thick slices galangal or fresh ginger
2 stalks lemongrass, cut into 2 in (5 cm) long pieces and bruised
4 kaffir lime leaves, torn in half (optional)
1 tablespoon palm or brown sugar
1½ teaspoons Roasted Red Chili Paste (page 23) or store-bought (nam prik pao, optional)
1 cup (250 ml) coconut milk
½ lb (250 g) boneless, skinless chicken thigh, cut into 1 in (2.5 cm) pieces
1 cup (70 g) sliced white button mushrooms
3 tablespoons freshly squeezed lime juice
2 tablespoons fish sauce (nam pla)
2–3 fresh hot red or green chilies, preferably Thai, smashed
Fresh coriander leaves (cilantro) for garnish

1 Put the chicken stock, galangal, lemongrass, kaffir lime leaves (if using) palm sugar, and Roasted Red Chili Paste (if using) in a medium saucepan and bring to a boil over medium heat.
2 Add the coconut milk, reduce the heat and bring to a simmer. Add the chicken and mushrooms and continue simmering until the chicken is white and opaque, 5–7 minutes.
3 Quickly stir in the lime juice and fish sauce. Float the chilies on the soup. Dish out into individual serving bowls and sprinkle with fresh coriander leaves. Serve immediately.

Chicken Coconut Soup

Sizzling Rice Seafood Soup

This soup is an ode to our Uncle Jack's famous Cantonese sizzling rice soup but with a Thai twist. I have so many fond memories as a child of sitting around a huge banquet table while a waiter placed the rice patties into the soup. All of the children would gasp as the rice would make the "sizzling" sound and we would clap with delight.

SERVES 4 AS PART OF A MULTI-COURSE
MEAL
PREPARATION TIME: 10 MINS
COOKING TIME: 20 MINS

½ cup (112 g) long-grain white rice, uncooked
1 tablespoon high-heat cooking oil
2 cloves garlic, minced
¼ small white onion, finely chopped
2 fresh hot red or green chilies, preferably Thai (deseeded if you prefer less heat), finely sliced
Six ¼ in (6 mm) thick slices galangal or fresh ginger
3 kaffir lime leaves, torn in half (optional)
12 medium shrimp, peeled and deveined
3 cups (750 ml) Basic Chicken Stock (page 26) or store-bought
½ teaspoon salt
½ lb (225 g) bay scallops
2 tablespoons fish sauce (nam pla)
¼ cup (62 ml) freshly squeezed lime juice
Oil for frying
Fresh Thai or Italian basil leaves for garnish

1 Wash the rice in cool water by rubbing rice gently between your fingers; drain. Repeat washing it until water is clear, 5 or 6 times; drain. Combine ¾ cups water (185 ml) and the rice in a medium, heavy-bottomed pot with a tight-fitting lid. Bring to a boil over high heat. As soon as the water is boiling, lower the heat to a simmer and cover. Cook at a gentle simmer until the water is completely absorbed and the rice is tender, about 12 minutes. Remove from heat and let sit for 5 minutes with lid on. Remove the lid and fluff with a fork and let cool.

2 While the rice is cooling, preheat oven to 300°F (150°C). Place the rice on a sheet pan, making sure that it is about, but no more than, ¼ inch (6 mm) thick. Bake the rice for 50–55 minutes, until it is dry. Cool and cut into 2 inch (5 cm) squares. Set aside.

3 Heat the oil in a stockpot over medium-high heat. Add the garlic, onions, and chilies and stir-fry until the garlic is fragrant and the onion is translucent, about 1 minute. Add the galangal, kaffir lime leaves (if using), and shrimp; stir-fry for 3–4 minutes. Add chicken stock, salt, and scallops, stir to combine. Quickly stir in the fish sauce and lime juice. Cover, reduce heat, and bring to a simmer for about 5 minutes. Keep warm on low heat.

4 In a wok or deep skillet, heat 2–3 inches (5–7.5 cm) of the oil to 350°F (175°C). Add the baked rice squares. Deep-fry until they puff and turn brown, then drain on a paper towel-lined sheet pan.

5 Dish out soup to a large serving bowl. Add the rice squares into the serving bowl at the dinner table so guests can hear the "popping" sound when they're added to the broth. Dish out to individual serving bowls and garnish with basil leaves. Serve immediately.

COOK'S NOTE: You may make the rice in a rice cooker on the regular setting if you prefer. Wash and drain rice and steam in rice cooker with ¾ cup (185 ml) water as instructed.

SERVES 4 AS PART OF A MULTI-COURSE
  MEAL
PREPARATION TIME: 10 MINUTES
COOKING TIME: 20 MINUTES

2 cups (500 ml) vegetable stock
1 cup (250 ml) coconut milk
1 teaspoon salt
1 tablespoon thick red curry paste
Six ¼ in (6 mm) thick slices galangal or
  fresh ginger
2 stalks lemongrass, cut into 2 in (5
  cm) long pieces and bruised
One 15 oz (425 g) can straw mushrooms, rinsed, drained, and halved
2 carrots, halved and thinly sliced
1 red bell pepper, thinly sliced
1 zucchini, thinly sliced
14 oz (400 g) extra-firm tofu, drained
  and cut into small cubes
½ cup (50 g) snow peas, tips and
  strings removed and sliced in half
  on a diagonal
2 tablespoons freshly squeezed lime
  juice
Fresh coriander leaves (cilantro) for
  garnish
Fresh Thai or Italian basil leaves for
  garnish

1 Bring the stock, coconut milk, and salt to a boil in a pot over medium-high heat.
2 Add the curry paste, stirring to break up the paste, about 1 minute. Add the galangal, lemongrass, mushrooms, carrots, red pepper, and zucchini and bring to a boil. Reduce to medium low heat and simmer until just tender, 3–5 minutes.
3 Add the tofu and snow peas and simmer until the snow peas are bright green, about 1 minute.
4 Quickly stir in the lime juice. Dish out into individual serving bowls and sprinkle with fresh coriander and basil leaves. Serve immediately.

Vegetable and Tofu Soup

I love all the fresh and tender-crisp veggies in this soup combined with the rich flavors from the coconut milk and curry paste. It makes me feel healthy just eating it yet knowing I'll be able to power through my day with its generous serving of tofu. My vegetarian friend Randi always texts me on her way to my house saying "you're making that yummy curry soup for me, right?"

Tangy Pumpkin Soup

It was really cool to check out the pumpkins while we were in Thailand because they're so different from the American kind with their dark grey or green skins. I learned not to judge a pumpkin by its cover because they're all sweet and delicious on the inside. Thais often use pumpkins to make desserts or delicious savory soups like this one. The heat from the spices is a great contrast to the sweet pumpkin in this seasonal soup. You may substitute the pumpkin with any kind of winter squash.

SERVES 4 OR 6 AS PART OF A MULTI-COURSE MEAL
PREPARATION TIME: 15 MINUTES
COOKING TIME: 25 MINUTES

2 tablespoons high-heat cooking oil
1 clove garlic, chopped
4 tablespoons finely chopped shallots
¼ teaspoon turmeric
½ teaspoon ground coriander
½ teaspoon cumin
2 fresh hot red or green chilies, preferably Thai (deseeded if you prefer less heat), thinly sliced
3 cups (750 ml) Basic Chicken Stock (page 26) or store-bought
2 stalks lemongrass, cut into 2 in (5 cm) long pieces and bruised
1 teaspoon palm or brown sugar
1 teaspoon salt
4 cups (700 g) peeled and diced pumpkin
1 cup (250 ml) coconut milk
2 tablespoons fish sauce (nam pla)
1 tablespoon freshly squeezed lime juice
Fresh Thai or Italian basil leaves for garnish

1 Heat the oil and butter in a pot over medium-high heat. Stir-fry the garlic, shallots, turmeric, coriander, cumin, and chilies until fragrant, about 1 minute. Add the chicken stock, lemongrass, palm sugar, salt, pumpkin, and coconut milk. Stir to combine and bring to a boil. Cook until the pumpkin softens, about 8–10 minutes. Quickly stir in fish sauce and lime juice.
2 Transfer to a blender or using an immersion hand blender, blend the soup to a smooth or slightly chunky consistency, depending on preference. Dish out into your individual serving bowls and sprinkle with basil leaves. Serve immediately.

Sour Spicy Shrimp Soup
(Tom Yum Goong)

Many Thai restaurants in the U.S. make Tom Yum Goong with chicken stock, but in Thailand this soup is made strictly with water, which I think creates a much brighter and cleaner flavor to complement the shrimp.

SERVES 4 AS PART OF A MULTI-COURSE MEAL
PREPARATION TIME: 10 MINUTES
COOKING TIME: 20 MINUTES

3 cups (750 ml) water
4 kaffir lime leaves, torn in half (optional)
Six ¼ in (6 mm) thick slices galangal or fresh ginger
2 stalks lemongrass, cut into 2 in (5 cm) long pieces and bruised
One 15 oz (425 g) can straw mushrooms, rinsed, drained, and halved
3 tablespoons fish sauce (nam pla)
2 tablespoons freshly squeezed lime juice
1 fresh hot red or green chili pepper, preferably Thai,
    (deseeded if you prefer less heat), thinly sliced
6 cherry or grape tomatoes, halved
1 tablespoon Roasted Red Chili Paste (page 23)
    or store-bought (nam prik pao, optional)
12 medium-sized shrimp, peeled and deveined
Fresh coriander leaves (cilantro) for garnish

1 Bring water, kaffir lime leaves (if using), galangal, and lemongrass to a boil over medium heat.
2 Add the mushrooms, fish sauce, and lime juice. Cook slowly and uncovered for 5 minutes. Add the chili and tomatoes and cook for 5 more minutes. Remove from heat. Add the shrimp and let stand for 4–5 minutes until shrimp is cooked through, stirring gently. Stir in the Roasted Red Chili Paste, if using, before serving. Remove from heat.
3 Dish out into your individual serving bowls and sprinkle with fresh coriander leaves. Serve immediately.

COOK'S NOTE: You could easily create a vegetarian version of this recipe by using tofu in place of the shrimp; soy sauce in place of the fish sauce and omitting the Roasted Red Chili Paste.

Sour Spicy Shrimp Soup

Hot and Sour Chicken Soup
(Tom Yum Gai)

"Sublime" is the best word to describe this quintessential Thai soup with its perfect balance of sweet, hot, salty, and sour flavors. I first had this soup while visiting my brother in Chicago where our late mother took us for our first gourmet Thai restaurant experience at Arun's. I've been hooked ever since.

SERVES 4 AS PART OF A MULTI-COURSE MEAL
PREPARATION TIME: 10 MINUTES
COOKING TIME: 20 MINUTES

3 cups (750 ml) Basic Chicken Stock (page 26) or store-bought
4 kaffir lime leaves, torn in half (optional)
Six ¼ in (6 mm) thick slices galangal or fresh ginger
2 stalks lemongrass, cut into 2 in (5 cm) long pieces and bruised
½ lb (250 g) boneless, skinless chicken thigh, cut into 1 in (2.5 cm) pieces
One 15 oz (425 g) can straw mushrooms, rinsed, drained, and halved
3 tablespoons fish sauce (nam pla)
2 tablespoons freshly squeezed lime juice
1 fresh hot red or green chili popper, preferably Thai, (deseeded if you prefer less heat), thinly sliced
6 cherry or grape tomatoes, halved
1 teaspoon Roasted Red Chili Paste (page 23) or store-bought (nam prik pao, optional)
Fresh coriander leaves (cilantro) for garnish

1 Bring the stock, kaffir lime leaves, galangal, and lemongrass to a boil over medium heat in a medium pot.
2 Add the chicken, mushrooms, fish sauce, and lime juice. Cook slowly and uncovered for 10 minutes. Add the chili and tomatoes and cook for 5 more minutes. Stir in the Roasted Red Chili Paste (if using). Remove from the heat.
3 Dish out into your individual serving bowls and sprinkle with fresh coriander leaves. Serve immediately.

CHAPTER THREE
Salads

Achieving a harmonious balance of flavors and textures is the main philosophy in Thai cooking so it's no surprise that salads are an integral part of everyday eating. A cooling, crisp salad is the natural accompaniment to a hot and spicy curry dish. Everywhere you look in Thailand you see plates full of crisp lettuce to wrap a satay or spring roll or a vibrant handful of fresh coriander leaves (cilantro) waiting to be dropped into a hot and sour soup. Thais love their fresh, raw vegetables and salads are no exception.

Many of the salads in this chapter can be served as part of a multi-course meal or as a lunch entrée. I can't think of anything more sublime than a lazy Saturday lunch enjoying the glistening Roast Duck Salad (page 60) with a glass of Pinot Noir. The Green Papaya Crab Salad (Som Yum) (page 59), is wildly popular all over Thailand and once you make it you'll understand why. The Spicy Thai Salad with Minced Pork (page 54) is so simple, yet so flavorful from the richness of the pork intermingled with red onions and an unexpected crunch from the roasted rice powder. Once you try the citrusy, light and tender Lemongrass Chicken Salad (page 55), you'll never look back at your plain-grilled-chicken-salad-eating-past again. Elegant and simple, the Glass Noodle Salad with Shrimp and Basil (page 58) is light and refreshing, with just the right amount of heat from the chili-garlic sauce.

My husband's personal favorite is the Thai Steak Salad (page 63) where he puts his awesome grilling skills to use. He loves how we turn his simple grilled steak into a vibrant, hot, sour, sweet, and salty salad masterpiece.

Spicy Thai Salad with Minced Pork (Larb)

Larb or laab is traditionally served wrapped in lettuce leaves, but here, greens are incorporated as a mixed salad. I did the happy dance in my kitchen when I made this after being inspired by the *larb* I sampled on my last trip to Thai Town with my friend, Stacy. It is hands down one of the best salads I've ever tasted. I just can't get enough of the zing from the red onions, richness from the pork and crunch from the toasted rice powder. All this marries beautifully with the sweet, salty, sour, and spicy flavors from the lime juice, chili, and fish sauce.

SERVES 4 AS PART OF MULTI-COURSE MEAL OR FOR LUNCH
PREPARATION TIME: 20 MINUTES + COOLING TIME
COOKING TIME: 30 MINUTES

1 tablespoon long-grain rice
1 tablespoon high-heat cooking oil
1 garlic clove, minced
1 small shallot, finely sliced
1 teaspoon minced lemongrass
1 fresh hot red or green chili, preferably Thai (deseeded if you prefer less heat)
½ lb (250 g) ground pork
3 tablespoons Basic Chicken Stock (page 26) or store-bought
2 tablespoons fish sauce (nam pla)
3 tablespoons freshly squeezed lime juice
1 tablespoon palm or brown sugar
4 cups (350 g) mixed baby greens
1 red pepper, thinly sliced
½ cup (52 g) peeled, seeded, and diced cucumber
12–14 fresh mint leaves
2 tablespoons finely chopped fresh coriander leaves (cilantro)
2 tablespoons finely chopped fresh Thai or Italian basil
½ small red onion, thinly sliced
4 tablespoons crushed roasted peanuts
Fresh coriander leaves (cilantro) for garnish
Mint leaves for garnish
Lime wedges

1 Make the roasted rice powder: Heat the rice in a small dry skillet over medium heat, stirring and tossing for 3–4 minutes, until it turns golden brown. Transfer to a small plate and allow to cool. Use a mortar and pestle or a spice grinder and grind the rice into a coarse powder.
2 Heat the oil in a wok or skillet on medium-high heat. Add garlic, shallots, lemongrass, and chili; stir-fry until fragrant, about 30 seconds. Add pork and stir-fry, while breaking it up with a wooden spoon until cooked through, about 5–6 minutes. Stir in the chicken stock, fish sauce, lime juice, and palm sugar and bring to a boil. Remove from heat and let stand 10 minutes.
3 In a large bowl, combine the rice powder, baby greens, mint leaves, fresh coriander leaves, basil, and red onions. Add the warm pork mixture and toss with the greens. Sprinkle crushed peanuts on top. Garnish with fresh coriander and mint leaves. Serve immediately with lime wedges.

COOK'S NOTE: Feel free to substitute the fish sauce with soy sauce, the pork with soy protein crumbles and the chicken stock with vegetable stock for a vegetarian version of this salad.

Lemongrass Chicken Salad

Why have the same old grilled chicken salad when you can dress it up with refreshing lemongrass tossed in an exotic combination of green beans, coconut, red cabbage, and herbs? Not only is this salad remarkably tasty, it is gorgeous and colorful. Yard-long beans are found at most Asian markets but it's totally fine to use fresh green beans in this salad.

SERVES 4 AS PART OF MULTI-COURSE MEAL OR FOR LUNCH
PREPARATION TIME: 20 MINUTES + MARINATING TIME
COOKING TIME: 14 MINUTES

2 boneless, skinless chicken breasts
   or thighs

MARINADE
2 teaspoons soy sauce
1 tablespoon fish sauce (nam pla)
1 tablespoon palm or brown sugar
1½ tablespoons minced lemongrass
1 garlic clove, minced
2 tablespoons dark sesame oil

DRESSING
2 teaspoons minced galangal or
   fresh ginger
2 teaspoons palm or brown sugar
2 tablespoons fresh lime juice
2 tablespoons fish sauce (nam pla)
½ teaspoon Asian chili-garlic sauce,
   preferably sambal oelek
4 tablespoons oil
1 teaspoon olive or canola oil

SALAD
6 yard-long beans or 12 green beans,
   cut into 2 in (5 cm) pieces
1 cup (71 g) shredded coconut
2 cups (152 g) red cabbage sliced into
   thin shreds/threads
4 tablespoons crushed roasted peanuts
4 tablespoons finely chopped fresh
   coriander leaves (cilantro)
4 tablespoons finely chopped mint
4 tablespoons finely chopped basil
½ small red onion, thinly sliced
6 kaffir lime leaves, thinly sliced
   (optional)

1 Marinade: In a small bowl, whisk together the soy sauce, fish sauce palm sugar, lemongrass, garlic, and sesame oil. Place the chicken in a large, resealable plastic food bag and marinate for 1 hour (up to overnight) in the refrigerator.

2 Preheat broiler. Remove the chicken from the marinade. Broil for 7 minutes per side. Transfer to a cutting board and let stand for 5 minutes. Cut the chicken into thin slices.

3 Dressing: In a small bowl, whisk together the galangal, palm sugar, lime juice, fish sauce, and chili-garlic sauce. Gradually whisk together the ingredients for the Dressing.

4 Salad: Cook the beans in boiling water until tender-crisp, about 5 minutes. Using a slotted spoon, transfer beans to an ice bath until cool. Drain and set aside.

5 Combine the reserved beans, coconut, cabbage, peanuts, fresh coriander leaves, mint, basil, onion, and kaffir lime leaves, if using, in a large bowl. Divide the Salad evenly on 4 plates. Divide the chicken pieces evenly among the salads. Drizzle the remaining Dressing on top of the chicken. Serve immediately.

Spicy Crispy Calamari Salad

Not only is this salad amazingly delicious, it's also a looker. Delicate and crispy calamari perched atop mixed greens glistening in an herb-spiked vinaigrette is a wonderful sight. When my fashion maven friend, Christos, tried it he said, "Darling, this salad is dressed to the nines!" The combination of textures can't be beat and will have your guests whispering out loud, "How does she do it?" Make sure to serve this salad while the calamari is still crispy for best results. I love to pair this salad with a light sparkling wine or champagne.

SERVES 4 AS PART OF MULTI-COURSE MEAL OR FOR LUNCH
PREPARATION TIME: 25 MINUTES
COOKING TIME: 10 MINUTES

1 cup (130 g) flour
1 cup (128 g) all-purpose cornstarch
1/8 teaspoon ground red pepper (cayenne)
1/8 teaspoon five spice powder
Pinch of salt and freshly ground black pepper
1 lb (500 g) calamari, cleaned and cut into 1/2 in (1.25 cm) rings
Oil for frying
Salt and pepper to taste

DRESSING
2 tablespoons fresh lime juice
2 tablespoons fish sauce
2 teaspoons minced lemongrass
1 tablespoon palm or brown sugar
1/2 teaspoon crushed red pepper flakes
2 tablespoon finely chopped fresh coriander leaves (cilantro)
2 tablespoons finely chopped fresh mint
3 tablespoons oil
1 tablespoon olive or canola oil

SALAD
1/2 cup (90 g) cherry or grape tomatoes, halved
4 tablespoons finely chopped fresh coriander leaves (cilantro))
4 tablespoons finely chopped fresh Thai or Italian basil
1 small carrot, cut into matchsticks
3 cups (260 g) mixed baby greens
Fresh coriander leaves (cilantro) for garnish

1 Combine the flour, ground red pepper, five spice powder, salt, and pepper in a medium bowl. In a large wok or deep skillet, heat 2–3 inches (5–7.3 cm) of oil to 350ºF (175°). Toss the calamari in the seasoned flour mixture. Shake excess flour off the calamari and fry in the oil until golden brown, about 1 minute. Remove with a metal strainer and allow it to drain on a paper towel-lined sheet pan. Season the calamari to taste with salt and pepper. Set aside.
2 Dressing: In a small bowl, whisk together lime juice, fish sauce, lemongrass, palm sugar, red pepper flakes, fresh coriander leaves, and mint. Gradually whisk in the olive oil and sesame oil until well blended.
3 Salad: In a large serving bowl, combine tomatoes, fresh coriander leaves, basil, carrots, and baby greens. Add all but 2 tablespoons of Dressing and toss to combine. Arrange calamari on top of the Salad. Drizzle the remaining Dressing over the calamari. Garnish with fresh coriander leaves. Serve immediately.

COOK'S NOTE: Don't overcook the calamari or it will become rubbery.

Mango and Prawn Salad

Tall and tan and young and lovely makes me think of this salad or how I imagine myself eating it on a lounge chair basking on a beach in Thailand (although I am neither tall, tan, or young!). A girl can dream, can't she? Whether you're sitting in a snow storm in Minnesota or enjoying a sunny day in Miami, this delicious and bright salad will transport you to a tropical beach in Thailand bursting with bright and sunny flavors from the mango and lime juice balanced with just enough heat from the chili sauce and yummy crunchiness from the veggies and peanuts.

SERVES 4 AS PART OF MULTI-COURSE MEAL OR FOR LUNCH
PREPARATION TIME: 20 MINUTES

DRESSING
2 teaspoons minced galangal or fresh ginger
2 teaspoons palm or brown sugar
2 tablespoons freshly squeezed lime juice
2 tablespoons fish sauce (nam pla)
½ teaspoon Asian chili-garlic sauce, preferably sambal oelek
¼ cup olive or canola oil
1 teaspoon dark sesame oil

SALAD
16 cooked medium-sized shrimp, peeled and deveined
1 cup (165 g) sliced fresh mango
½ cup (52 g) chopped cucumber, peeled and seeded
½ cup (46 g) chopped red bell pepper
4 tablespoons finely chopped fresh coriander leaves (cilantro)
4 tablespoons crushed roasted peanuts
Mixed baby greens for four salad plates

1 Dressing: In a small bowl, whisk together the Dressing ingredients. Gradually whisk in olive oil and sesame oil until well blended.
2 In a large bowl, combine shrimp, mango, cucumber, red pepper, fresh coriander leaves, and peanuts. Add the Dressing and toss to combine. Divide salad greens evenly among four plates. Place salad mixture on top of greens. Serve immediately.

Glass Noodle Salad with Shrimp and Basil

Glass noodles are also known as cellophane noodles, Chinese vermicelli or dried mung bean noodles. They're actually made from mung bean starch and are translucent once hydrated, hence the nickname "glass." The glass is definitely half full here as this salad is incredibly, light, healthy, and delicious.

SERVES 4 AS PART OF MULTI-COURSE MEAL OR FOR LUNCH

PREPARATION TIME: 20 MINUTES + SOAKING TIME

DRESSING
- 1 clove garlic, minced
- ½ teaspoon Asian chili-garlic sauce, preferably sambal oelek
- 2 tablespoons minced lemongrass
- 4 tablespoons fish sauce (nam pla)
- 2 tablespoons freshly squeezed lime juice
- 1 tablespoon palm or brown sugar
- 3 tablespoons olive or canola oil
- 1 tablespoon dark sesame oil

SALAD
- 6 oz (175 g) dried glass noodles
- 1 teaspoon dark sesame oil
- 16 shelled and deveined small-sized cooked shrimp
- ½ cup (10 g) fresh Thai or Italian basil leaves, sliced
- 1 cucumber, peeled, deseeded and chopped
- 1 red bell pepper, thinly sliced
- ½ cup (50 g) finely chopped green onions (green and white parts)
- 1 small carrot, cut into matchsticks
- Fresh coriander leaves (cilantro) for garnish

1 Dressing: In a small bowl, whisk together the ingredients for the Dressing. Gradually whisk in the oil and sesame oil until well blended.

2 For the Salad, soak the noodles in freshly boiled water according to the package's directions. Once rehydrated, rinse with cool water and drain. Toss with 1 teaspoon sesame oil.

3 Combine the shrimp, reserved glass noodles, basil leaves, cucumber, red pepper, green onions, and carrots into a bowl. Add the Dressing and toss to combine. Garnish with fresh coriander leaves before serving. Serve immediately.

COOK'S NOTE: Don't confuse glass noodles with rice vermicelli which is made with rice flour and aren't clear when cooked. Look for "Chinese vermicelli" or "cellophane noodles" on the packaging.

How to Make Green Papaya Crab Salad

1 Shred the papaya into thin slices using a grater.

2 Gently pound the garlic and chilies into a paste.

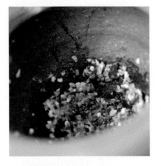

3 Add papaya and green beans.

4 Add remaining ingredients and toss well before serving.

Green Papaya Crab Salad

Green Papaya Crab Salad (Som Yum)

I'm madly in love with this salad, which is usually made with salted crab, but I use lump crabmeat in this recipe, which is a bit more user friendly. I tried this salad for the first time near Phang Nga Bay where they filmed the James Bond classic, *The Man with the Golden Gun*, and I discovered the amazing texture and flavor of unripe papaya. It's bold, pungent, spicy and a bit wild. Thais use a special tool to slice the papaya, which you may be able to find in a Thai market, but I used my food processor's shredding blade and it was sliced within seconds.

**SERVES 4 AS PART OF MULTI-COURSE MEAL OR FOR LUNCH
PREPARATION TIME: 25 MINUTES**

3 garlic cloves, coarsely chopped
1 fresh hot red or green chili, preferably Thai (deseeded if you prefer less heat), finely sliced
4 cups (400 g) green unripe papaya, sliced
6 yard-long beans or 12 fresh green beans, cut into 2 in (5 cm) pieces
2 tablespoons fish sauce (nam pla)
4 tablespoons freshly squeezed lime juice
2 tablespoons palm or brown sugar
1½ cups (270 g) cherry or grape tomatoes, halved
Two small handfuls of fresh coriander leaves (cilantro) (about ½ cup/24 g), finely chopped
12 oz (350 g) lump crab meat, picked over for shells
2 tablespoons crushed roasted peanuts plus more for garnish

1 Combine the garlic and chilies in a large mortar. Use the pestle to gently pound it into a coarse paste. Add the papaya and green beans and keep gently pounding and scraping until the papaya shreds start wilting and the beans are smashed. Now add the fish sauce, lime juice, and palm sugar. Press and combine with the pestle. Use a spoon to toss a bit if you wish. Transfer to a serving bowl.
2 Add the cherry tomatoes, crabmeat, and crushed peanuts to the mixture. Toss well and garnish with more crushed peanuts. Serve immediately.

Roast Duck Salad

Duck breasts are often sold frozen so I like to keep some on hand in my freezer to make this sumptuous salad. The glistening duck makes me feel luxurious, like a Thai Princess, until I look at my piles of laundry and am transported back to the suburbs. You can feel like royalty too with this rich and delicious salad.

SERVES 4 AS PART OF MULTI-COURSE MEAL OR FOR LUNCH
PREPARATION TIME: 20 MINUTES + MARINATING TIME
COOKING TIME: 15 MINUTES + COOLING TIME

2 boneless duck breast fillets

MARINADE
2 tablespoons freshly squeezed lime juice
2 garlic cloves, minced
1 tablespoon minced lemongrass
1 tablespoon palm or brown sugar
1 tablespoon fish sauce (nam pla)
2 teaspoons freshly ground black pepper
2 tablespoons dark sesame oil
1 teaspoon salt

DRESSING
4 tablespoons freshly squeezed lime juice
2 tablespoons honey
1 tablespoon rice or white vinegar
1 tablespoon fish sauce (nam pla)
2 teaspoons Asian chili-garlic sauce, preferably sambal oelek
1 teaspoon dark sesame oil
1 teaspoon finely chopped shallots

SALAD
4 cups (350 g) mixed baby greens
½ cup (48 g) snow peas, tips and strings removed and cut into thin matchsticks
1 cup (180 g) cherry or grape tomatoes, halved
4 tablespoons thinly sliced red onion
½ cup (46 g) thinly sliced red bell pepper
2 tablespoons finely chopped fresh coriander leaves (cilantro)
2 tablespoons finely chopped fresh mint

1 Marinade: In a small bowl, whisk together the lime juice, garlic, lemongrass, palm sugar, fish sauce, black pepper, sesame oil, and salt. Place duck breasts in a large resealable plastic food bag and marinate in the refrigerator for 1 hour (and up to 6 hours).

2 Preheat oven to 400°F (200°C). With a sharp knife score the fat side of the duck breasts in a criss-cross pattern. Warm a heavy bottomed ovenproof skillet over medium heat. Place the duck breasts, fat side down, in the skillet to render off the fat, about 6 minutes. Remove rendered duck fat. Turn the duck breasts over and sear for 1 minute. Turn the fat side down again and place the skillet into the oven to roast for 7–9 minutes, or until breasts are medium rare or to desired doneness. Let the duck breasts rest for 5 minutes. Remove skin and thinly slice.

3 Dressing: In a small bowl, whisk together lime juice, honey, vinegar, fish sauce, chili-garlic sauce, and shallots. Gradually whisk in sesame oil until well blended.

4 Bring a small saucepan of water to a boil. Add the snow peas and boil for 1 minute or until tender-crisp. Using a slotted spoon, transfer the snow peas to a bowl of ice water and let cool completely. Drain, and set aside.

5 Salad: In a large bowl, combine the baby greens, tomatoes, onion, red pepper, reserved snow peas, fresh coriander leaves, and mint. Add all but 2 tablespoons of Dressing and toss to combine. Divide the Salad evenly among 4 plates. Divide the duck evenly among the salads. Drizzle the remaining Dressing evenly over the top of the duck slices. Serve immediately.

Roast Duck Salad

Vegan Tofu Salad

Tofu is like a blank canvas and the seasonings you choose serve to dress up your work of art. Tofu absorbs all of the flavors around it so the bold flavors in this marinade meld beautifully in this vegan salad. I love the crunch from the snow peas, red pepper, carrots, cabbage and peanuts.

SERVES 4 AS PART OF MULTI-COURSE MEAL
PREPARATION TIME: 15 MINUTES + BLANCHING TIME

1 tablespoon homemade Sweet Thai Chili Sauce (page 24) or store-bought
1 fresh hot red or green chili, preferably Thai, deseeded and finely sliced
2 teaspoons minced galangal or fresh ginger
1 teaspoon minced lemongrass
1 clove garlic, minced
1½ tablespoons soy sauce
1 tablespoon dark sesame oil
12 oz (350 g) extra-firm tofu, drained and diced
1 cup (98 g) snow peas, tips and strings removed and cut into thin matchsticks
1 small red pepper, thinly sliced
1 small carrot, cut into thin matchsticks
1 cup (76 g) red cabbage, cut into thin shreads/threads
4 tablespoons crushed peanuts
Finely chopped green onions (green and white parts) for garnish

1 In a large bowl, whisk together the sweet chili sauce, chili, galangal, lemongrass, garlic, soy sauce, and sesame oil. Add the tofu to the mixture and toss to coat. Cover and marinate 1 hour in the refrigerator.
2 Bring a small saucepan of water to a boil. Add the snow peas and boil for 1 minute or until tender-crisp. Using a slotted spoon, transfer the snow peas to a bowl of ice water and let cool completely.
3 In a serving bowl, toss the snow peas, red pepper, carrots, cabbage, and peanuts with the tofu marinade mixture. Garnish with green onions and serve immediately.

Thai Steak Salad

When I'm entertaining in LA, I always make sure to include a low-carb option for those friends who shriek at the sight of a bread stick or fried rice (tsk, tsk…I know, how could I know such people? But hey, it's LA). This protein packed salad is flavorful and loaded with healthful spinach and herbs topped with a gorgeous grilled steak to satisfy anyone's appétit (and usually means more noodles for me!)

SERVES 4 AS PART OF MULTI-COURSE MEAL OR FOR LUNCH

1 lb (500 g) boneless rib eye steak
Salt
Freshly ground black pepper

DRESSING
2 tablespoons freshly squeezed lime juice
2 tablespoons soy sauce
2 tablespoons freshly squeezed orange juice
1½ teaspoons fish sauce (nam pla)
½ teaspoon Asian chili-garlic sauce, preferably sambal oelek
1 teaspoon minced lemongrass
1 clove garlic, minced
1 tablespoon dark sesame oil
1 tablespoon olive or canola oil

SALAD
1 cup (30 g) packed spinach leaves, stemmed and washed
1 cup (76 g) Napa cabbage, sliced into thin shreds/threads
¾ cup (21 g) fresh coriander leaves (cilantro)
⅓ cup (7 g) fresh Thai or Italian basil leaves, sliced
⅓ cup (7 g) fresh mint leaves
1 small carrot, cut into matchsticks
⅓ cup (55 g) diced fresh mango
Crushed roasted peanuts for garnish

1 Preheat the broiler. Season the steaks with salt and pepper. Broil for 4–7 minutes per side for medium-rare, or to the desired doneness. Transfer to a cutting board and let stand for 10 minutes, then cut across the grain into thin slices.
2 Dressing: In a small bowl, whisk together the Dressing ingredients. Gradually whisk in olive oil and sesame oil until well blended.
3 Salad: In a serving bowl, combine the spinach, cabbage, fresh coriander leaves, basil, mint, carrot, and mango. Add all but 2 tablespoons of dressing and toss to combine. Arrange the steak slices on top of Salad. Drizzle the remaining Dressing over the steak. Garnish with crushed peanuts and serve immediately.

CHAPTER FOUR

Poultry

My friend Jennifer called me the other day because she was stumped. Her husband was coming home with a new client in an hour and she had no idea what to do with the package of chicken staring back at her on her kitchen counter (with a baby on her hip, no less). If you're like most of my friends, you're always looking for new ways to cook chicken and it seems like there are no new ideas. Well, not anymore! Welcome to the wonderful world of Thai chicken. Thai people do wonderful things with chicken and it's no wonder as chickens are part of everyday life for many Thai people in villages or small towns where chickens roam free much like cats do in Greece.

Thai people are also legendary for their Thai BBQ Chicken (page 70). Sweet, hot, moist, and tender, it's the perfect BBQ dish and will make you the talk of the neighborhood. And the dipping sauce? Well, it's totally killer with intense flavors that will make your taste buds come alive. The classic Chicken with Cashews and Thai Chilies (page 66) is a flavor powerhouse and couldn't be simpler to make. You'll smile next time you see your local Thai take-out menu peeking out of your kitchen drawer knowing, "I can make that too!" Braised Chicken in Thai Yellow Curry (page 73) is a soul satisfying, hearty and rustic dish that you'll savor on a cool autumn night. Crispy, creamy, fruity, and tender, Crispy Mango Coconut Chicken (page 69) is a little more time consuming than other Thai dishes, but it's well worth the time and effort.

Let's not forget about duck. No Thai cookbook would be complete with Pineapple Duck Curry (page 75). The combination of red curry, duck and fresh pineapple is not only irresistible, it's completely addicting.

Chicken with Cashews and Thai Chilies

I first encountered this dish in Thai Town when I moved to LA; I loved the contrast between the sweetness of the cashews with the spicy dried peppers. When recreating this dish at home, I realized how fast and simple it is to make but, as with all stir-fries, it's important to have all of your ingredients prepped and ready to go as it cooks in mere minutes. If you can't find dried Thai peppers then it's fine to use Chiles de Arbol available at Hispanic markets and some grocery stores.

SERVES 2 AS A MAIN DISH WITH RICE OR 4 AS PART OF A MULTI-COURSE MEAL
PREPARATION TIME: 20 MINUTES
COOKING TIME: 15 MINUTES

10 oz (330 g) skinless, boneless chicken breast or chicken thigh, sliced crosswise thinly into ½ in (1.25 cm) wide strips
½ teaspoon all-purpose cornstarch
¼ teaspoon salt
Pinch of white pepper
2 tablespoons high-heat cooking oil
1 garlic clove, minced
1 small yellow onion, cut into cubes
4 dried Thai chilies or Chiles de Arbol
1½ teaspoons Roasted Red Chili Paste (page 23) or store-bought (nam prik pao, optional)
½ cup (125 ml) Basic Chicken Stock (page 26) or store-bought
2 teaspoons fish sauce (nam pla)
2 teaspoons soy sauce
1½ teaspoons sugar
½ cup (75 g) dry-roasted cashews
Finely chopped green onions for garnish

1 Toss the chicken with the all-purpose cornstarch, salt, and white pepper in a small bowl. Cover and refrigerate for 10 minutes.

2 Heat ½ of the oil in a wok or skillet over medium-high heat. Add the chicken and stir-fry until the chicken turns white. Remove the chicken from the pan and set aside. Wash and thoroughly dry the wok or skillet.

3 Heat the remaining oil in the wok or skillet over medium-high heat. Add the chilies and stir-fry for 1 minute. Remove the chilies with a slotted spoon and set aside. Add the garlic and onion to the wok or skillet, and stir-fry until fragrant, about 1 minute. Add the Roasted Red Chili Paste (if using) and stir-fry, stirring to break it up, about 1 minute.

4 Add the chicken stock, fish sauce, soy sauce, and sugar. Stir well and simmer for 3 minutes. Lower the heat to medium. Add the reserved chicken, cashews, and chilies; cook until the sauce is slightly thickened, about 4 minutes. Dish out and serve immediately with jasmine rice.

COOK'S NOTE: You can double the Roasted Red Chili Paste for extra heat and flavor.

Chicken with Cashews and Thai Chilies

Chicken with Mint and Thai Basil

My husband has the green thumb in our family so I love raiding his abundant garden where he's planted copious amounts of Thai herbs. Unlike Chinese stir-fries which use a lot of ginger, Thais like to use large quantities of aromatic herbs, like mint and basil, to flavor their dishes. Feel free to use Italian basil if you can't find Thai basil. This dish works great with shrimp, beef, or pork as well.

SERVES 2 AS A MAIN DISH WITH RICE OR 4 AS PART OF A MULTI-COURSE MEAL
PREPARATION TIME: 10 MINUTES
COOKING TIME: 8 MINUTES

10 oz (330 g) skinless, boneless chicken breast or chicken thigh, sliced crosswise thinly into ½ in (1.25 cm) wide strips
½ teaspoon all-purpose cornstarch
¼ teaspoon salt
Pinch of white pepper
2 tablespoons high-heat cooking oil
1 garlic clove, minced
1 small shallot, thinly sliced
1 fresh hot red or green chili, preferably Thai (deseeded if you prefer less heat), thinly sliced
2 kaffir lime leaves, finely sliced (optional)
2 teaspoons soy sauce
2 teaspoons fish sauce (nam pla)
1½ teaspoons sugar
¾ cup (15 g) fresh Thai or Italian basil leaves
¾ cup (15 g) fresh mint leaves

1 Toss the chicken with the all-purpose cornstarch and salt in small bowl. Cover and refrigerate for 10 minutes.
2 Heat ½ of the oil in a wok or skillet over medium-high heat. Add the chicken and stir-fry until the chicken turns white. Remove the chicken from the pan and set aside.
3 Heat the remaining oil in the wok or skillet over medium-high heat. Add the garlic, shallots and chilies to the wok or skillet and stir-fry until fragrant, about 1 minute. Add the reserved chicken, kaffir lime leaves (if using), soy sauce, fish sauce, and sugar; stir-fry for 2 minutes or until the chicken is cooked through. Add the basil and mint leaves and stir-fry for about 30 seconds or until the basil is wilted. Dish out and serve immediately with jasmine rice.

How to Make the Crispy Mango Coconut Chicken

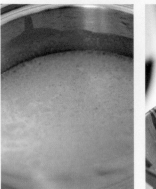

1 Prepare the marinade for the chicken by mixing together the egg, salt, pepper, and ginger.

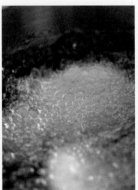

2 After the sauce ingredients come to a boil, stir in the cornstarch mixture and cook until thickened, about 10 seconds.

3 Place the prepared batter and marinated chicken near your stove top in preparation for frying.

4 One at a time, dip the chicken pieces into the batter to coat all sides.

5 Heat oil to 350°F (175°C) and fry a few pieces at a time for about 3 minutes, turning 2 or 3 times until light brown.

6 Fry the chicken pieces again until golden brown, about 2 minutes.

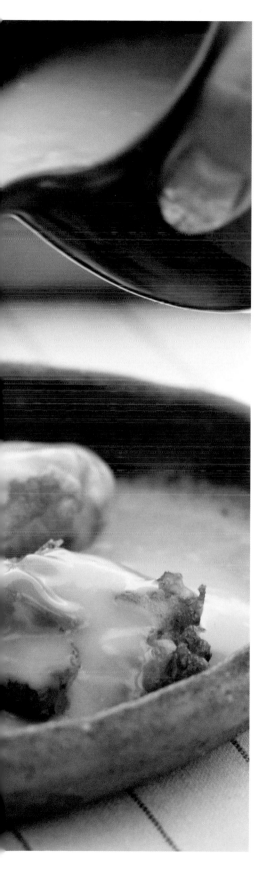

Crispy Mango Coconut Chicken

This recipe is in memory of my late mother, Leeann, an incredible chef and restaurateur. Her crispy chicken was legendary and I use her batter recipe for this dish. It's incredibly light and crispy on the outside, moist and juicy on the inside. The mango coconut sauce is smooth and creamy and is laced with just the right amount of fruity mango goodness.

SERVES 4 AS PART OF A MULTI-COURSE MEAL
PREPARATION TIME: 15 MINUTES + MARINATING TIME
COOKING TIME: 20 MINUTES

1 lb (500 g) skinless, boneless chicken breast
1 large egg
2 teaspoons + 2 tablespoons all-purpose cornstarch, divided
1¼ teaspoons salt, divided
¼ teaspoon white pepper
1 teaspoon peeled and minced fresh ginger
¼ cup (32 g) all-purpose flour
¼ cup (65 ml) water
2 tablespoons oil
¼ teaspoon baking soda
Oil for frying

MANGO COCONUT SAUCE
1 tablespoon high-heat cooking oil
1 garlic clove, minced
¾ cup (185 ml) Basic Chicken Stock (page 26) or store-bought
¾ cup (185 ml) coconut milk
¼ cup (65 ml) puréed mango
2 tablespoons freshly squeezed lime juice
¼ cup (50 g) sugar
2 tablespoons rice or white vinegar
2 tablespoons all-purpose cornstarch mixed with 2 tablespoons water

1 Cut the chicken in half lengthwise and pound to flatten the thick part so the chicken is of consistent thickness. Place the chicken in a shallow dish. In a small bowl, mix together the egg, 2 teaspoons all-purpose cornstarch, 1 teaspoon salt, the pepper and the ginger. Pour the egg mixture over the chicken, turning the chicken to coat all sides. Cover and refrigerate 30 minutes. Remove the chicken from the marinade. Reserve the marinade.

2 Mango Coconut Sauce: In a small saucepan, heat the oil over medium-high heat. Add the garlic and stir-fry until fragrant, about 30 seconds. Add the chicken stock, coconut milk, puréed mango, lime juice, sugar, and vinegar; bring to a boil. Stir in the all-purpose cornstarch mixture. Cook and stir until thickened, about 10 seconds. Remove from heat.

3 In a shallow dish, mix the reserved marinade, flour, water, the remaining 2 tablespoons cornstarch, oil, baking soda, and the remaining ¼ teaspoon salt.

4 In a wok or deep skillet, heat 2–3 inches (5–7.5 cm) of the oil to 350°F. One at a time, dip the chicken pieces into the batter to coat all sides. Fry the chicken pieces for about 3 minutes, or until light brown, turning 2–3 times. Increase the oil temperature to 375°F (175°C). Fry the chicken pieces again until golden brown, turning once, about 2 minutes, and drain on a paper towel-lined sheet pan. Using a very sharp knife, cut each piece of chicken crosswise into ¾ inch (2 cm) pieces. Transfer the chicken pieces to a serving platter. Reheat the sauce over medium-high heat and pour over the chicken. Serve immediately.

Thai BBQ Chicken (Gai Yaang)

When I used to cater in the Hamptons during the summers, my clients would go crazy for this tangy and sticky BBQ chicken with sweet heat. Gai Yaang is a common street food in Thailand and it's easy to see why it's so popular. Make it for your next BBQ and I guarantee your friends will be begging you to make it again. You may want to double the sauce as it's addicting and great to have on hand to drizzle over leftovers.

SERVES 4 AS PART OF A MULTI-COURSE MEAL
PREPARATION TIME: 10 MINUTES + MARINATING TIME
COOKING TIME: 50 MINUTES

4 bone-in chicken quarters with skin on

BBQ MARINADE
8 garlic cloves, minced
1 tablespoon freshly ground black pepper
3 tablespoons fish sauce (nam pla)
2 tablespoons cooking sherry
1 tablespoon dark sesame oil
4 tablespoons palm or brown sugar
2 tablespoons minced lemongrass
1 fresh hot red or green chili, preferably Thai (deseeded if you prefer less heat), finely sliced
2 tablespoons honey

DIPPING SAUCE
½ cup (125 ml) rice or white vinegar
⅓ cup (56 g) palm or brown sugar
1 tablespoon finely chopped shallots.
1½ teaspoons Asian chili sauce, preferably Sriracha
1 tablespoon fish sauce (nam pla)

1 BBQ Marinade: Whisk together the garlic, pepper, fish sauce, sherry, sesame oil, palm sugar, lemongrass, chili, and honey. Place the chicken in a large sealable plastic bag. Pour the marinade over the chicken. Place in the refrigerator for at least 2 hours (up to overnight).

2 Dipping Sauce: Bring vinegar, palm sugar, shallots, chili sauce, and fish sauce to a boil in a small sauce pan over high heat, stirring to combine. Reduce heat to medium low and allow to simmer for 10–15 minutes. Remove from heat.

3 Heat a grill to medium and brush with oil. Place the chicken on the grill skin side down and grill for about 15 minutes. Brush the uncooked side with the BBQ Marinade then flip the chicken over. Grill the second side for about 15 minutes. Discard the marinade. When the chicken is cooked through, transfer it to a serving platter and serve with the Dipping Sauce.

COOK'S NOTE: Keep a spray bottle filled with water near by when grilling to prevent flare ups.

Phuket Chicken with Lemongrass Curry

I remember strolling the sandy shores of Patong Beach in Phuket on our honeymoon and coming across a quaint beachside café that served the most delicious green curry lemongrass chicken dish, a culinary memory that inspires this recipe. Although curry originated in central Thailand it is used throughout the country. Green curry paste is made with green chilies and is similar in heat to thick red curry paste.

SERVES 4 WITH RICE AS PART OF A MULTI-COURSE MEAL
PREPARATION TIME: 10 MINUTES
COOKING TIME: 15 MINUTES

2 tablespoons high-heat cooking oil, divided
1 teaspoon green curry paste
2 cloves garlic, minced
1 tablespoon finely chopped shallots
4 tablespoons minced lemongrass
1 fresh hot red or green chili, preferably Thai (deseeded if you prefer less heat), finely sliced
1½ tablespoons fish sauce (nam pla)
1 teaspoon freshly ground black pepper
½ teaspoon palm or brown sugar
10 oz (330 g) skinless, boneless chicken thigh, cut into cubes
½ cup (125 ml) Basic Chicken Stock (page 26) or store-bought
1 cup (250 ml) coconut milk
3 tablespoons finely chopped fresh coriander leaves (cilantro)
Crushed roasted peanuts

1 Heat ½ of the oil in a wok or skillet over medium heat. Add the curry paste, stirring to break up paste, about 1 minute. Increase heat to medium-high. Add the garlic, shallots, lemongrass, and chili and stir-fry until fragrant, about 30 seconds. Add the fish sauce, pepper and palm sugar; stir-fry about 1 minute. Add remaining oil and the chicken and stir-fry for 3–4 minutes. Add the chicken stock and coconut milk.
2 Bring to a boil then reduce heat immediately to medium-low. Simmer for 4–5 minutes or until chicken is cooked through.
3 Add fresh coriander leaves and stir to combine. Dish out and serve immediately with jasmine rice. Garnish with peanuts.

Phuket Chicken with Lemongrass Curry

Braised Chicken in Thai Yellow Curry

After our twins were born, I used to make tons of this curry and keep it on hand when we were too exhausted to cook (most nights) and for the endless trail of friends who came to see our bundles of "double happiness." The amount of curry paste you'd like to use is up to you, but I recommend enough in this recipe for medium heat. Feel free to reduce or increase depending on your heat threshold. I recommend Mae Ploy or Maesri brands.

SERVES 6 AS A MAIN DISH WITH RICE AS PART OF A MULTI-COURSE MEAL
PREPARATION TIME: 5 MINUTES
COOKING TIME: 40 MINUTES

2 tablespoons high-heat cooking oil
2 lbs (1 kg) bone-in chicken thighs and chicken legs
3 tablespoons yellow curry paste or 3 tablespoons thick red curry paste mixed with 1 teaspoon curry powder
2 cups (500 ml) coconut milk
1 cup (250 ml) Basic Chicken Stock (page 26)
2 tablespoons fish sauce (nam pla)
2 tablespoon freshly squeezed lime juice
2 teaspoons palm or brown sugar

1 In a large skillet or dutch oven, heat the oil over medium-high heat. Brown the chicken pieces in batches until golden brown on all sides. Transfer the chicken to a large bowl.
2 Reduce heat to medium. Add curry paste, stirring to break it up, about 1 minute. Add the chicken pieces (along with its juices) to pan. Add coconut milk and chicken stock, stirring to coat chicken. Bring to a gentle boil, reduce heat, cover and simmer 15–20 minutes or until chicken is tender and cooked through. Stir in fish sauce, lime juice, and palm sugar. Dish out and serve immediately with jasmine rice.

SERVES 2 AS A MAIN DISH WITH RICE OR
4 AS PART OF A MULTI-COURSE MEAL
PREPARATION TIME: 20 MINUTES
COOKING TIME: 10 MINUTES

10 oz (330) skinless, boneless chicken breast or chicken thigh, sliced crosswise thinly into ½ in (1.25 cm) wide strips
½ teaspoon all-purpose cornstarch
¼ teaspoon salt
Pinch of white pepper
2 tablespoons high-heat cooking oil, divided
1 tablespoon thick red curry paste
1 garlic clove, minced
1 tablespoon minced galangal or fresh ginger
1 cup (110 g) fresh French green beans, cut into 2 in (5 cm) pieces
1 cup (250 ml) water
2 teaspoons fish sauce (nam pla)
2 kaffir lime leaves, cut into thin strips (optional)
1 tablespoon palm or brown sugar
Thai or Italian basil leaves for garnish

1 Toss the chicken with the all-purpose cornstarch, salt and white pepper in small bowl. Cover and refrigerate for 10 minutes.
2 Heat ½ of the oil in a wok or skillet over moderately high heat. Add the chicken and stir-fry until it turns white. Remove the chicken from pan and set aside. Wash and thoroughly dry the wok and skillet.
3 Heat the remaining oil in the wok or skillet over medium. Add the curry paste and stir-fry, stirring to break it up, about 1 more minute. Increase heat to medium-high. Add the garlic and ginger to the wok or skillet and stir-fry until fragrant, about 30 seconds. Add the green beans and water and cook until green beans are tender, about 5 minutes, stirring to combine with the paste. Add the reserved chicken, fish sauce, kaffir lime leaves, if using, and palm sugar; stir-fry for 30 seconds. Garnish with basil leaves, Dish out and serve with hot jasmine rice. Serve immediately.

Chicken with Curry Paste and French Green Beans
(Chicken Prik King)

Chicken Prik-King is a classic Thai dish fit for a King (or a Queen). It's incredibly easy to make but bursting with flavor. Double the amount of curry paste for more intense heat. The food in Thailand is much spicier than what you encounter at Thai restaurants in America. I remember having this dish in Bangkok and my forehead alone made it a three napkin affair! You could use shrimp, beef, or pork in this dish or a combination.

Pineapple Duck Curry

There's just something magical about the combination of pineapple, duck and red curry which explains why it's one of the most popular Thai curries. The spiciness of the garlic, chili and curry is tempered by the creamy coconut milk and sweet pineapple. As this dish calls for pre-roasted Chinese duck, you can get dinner on the table in a matter of minutes. Look for a Chinese deli in your local Chinatown or Asian neighborhood which has ducks hanging in the window. I always head to Sam Woo in LA for my roast ducks. For a bright finish, squeeze a wedge of fresh lime over it before serving.

SERVES 6 AS A MAIN DISH WITH RICE AS PART OF A MULTI-COURSE MEAL
PREPARATION TIME: 10 MINUTES
COOKING TIME: 15 MINUTES

1 tablespoon high-heat cooking oil
1 garlic clove, minced
1 teaspoon minced galangal or fresh ginger
1 fresh hot red or green chili, preferably Thai (deseeded for less heat), finely sliced
3 tablespoons thick red curry paste
2 tablespoons fish sauce (nam pla)
2 tablespoons palm or brown sugar
2 kaffir lime leaves, torn in half (optional)
8 oz (250 g) roast Chinese duck, thinly sliced
1 Asian eggplant, cut ½ lengthwise and then sliced crosswise into wedges
2 cups (500 ml) coconut milk
1 cup (250 ml) Basic Chicken Stock (page 26) or store-bought
1½ cups (337 g) diced fresh pineapple
8 small cherry or grape tomatoes, halved
4 tablespoons fresh Thai or Italian basil leaves
4 tablespoons fresh coriander leaves (cilantro)
4 tablespoons fresh mint leaves

1 Heat the oil in a skillet over medium-high heat. Add the garlic and ginger and stir-fry until fragrant, about 30 seconds. Reduce heat to medium and add the thick red curry paste, stirring to break it up, about 1 minute. Add the fish sauce, palm sugar, and kaffir lime leaves, if using, and cook for 2 minutes, while stirring to combine.
2 Add the duck, eggplant, and coconut milk and bring to a gentle boil. Reduce heat to medium-low and simmer for 5 minutes. Add the pineapple and cherry tomatoes, simmer for 2 more minutes. Add the basil, fresh coriander leaves, and mint leaves; cook for 30 seconds or until basil is wilted. Dish out and serve immediately with jasmine rice.

CHAPTER FIVE

Beef, Pork, and Lamb

I love Thai food because there's something for everyone. I feel like I can satisfy all of my friend's and family's appetites when I entertain because there are so many great vegetarian and gluten-free options, but there's also an amazing variety of seafood, poultry, and delicious meat dishes. Even my niece's "I only eat meat and potatoes" boyfriend from Iowa fell in love with the Thai meat dishes I was testing.

Beef is less abundant than seafood, chicken, or pork in Thai cuisine but that doesn't mean it doesn't get the royal Thai treatment. Most of the beef dishes in this chapter were influenced by other countries as is the case with many classic Thai dishes. In the rustic Northeastern province of Issan, Shaking Beef (page 81) is a garlicky, peppery melt-in-your-mouth dish served over greens brought to the region by Vietnamese immigrants. Panaeng Beef Curry (page 83), which originated on the west coast of Malaysia, is a milder, curry with savory spices simmered with tender crisp sugar snap peas and carrots. Beef with Red Chili Paste and Lime Leaves (page 87) is a classic Thai stir-fry dish with Chinese origins and is feisty and full of flavor.

In Thailand, pork is so integral to their cuisine that the word for pork and the word for meat are often interchangeable. Like chickens, pigs stroll the streets of villages and countryside. Versatile and flavorful, pork is used for a myriad of dishes from grilled to stir-fried to minced and braised. Chiang Mai Pork Curry (page 84) is a classic dish from this Northern Province which is a slow simmered dish unlike most Thai curries and is punctuated with a bright note of lime and finished with crushed roasted peanuts. Stir-fried Pork with Spicy Green Beans (page 79) is made with minced pork and is one of the simplest dishes to make as is Thai BBQ Pork (page 78)—both are easy weeknight go-to recipes for me.

Crying Tiger is a popular dish known for its heat (known to make a tiger howl) which is typically made with beef but I decided to switch it up with lamb loin chops for Crying Tiger Lamb (page 85). Tissues are optional.

Thai BBQ Pork

Thai BBQ pork couldn't be easier to make because you just throw all the marinade ingredients in a bag and go about your day. The flavors permeate the pork tenderloin nicely in this dish and the sweet Thai chili sauce is a terrific accompaniment to the spicy, salty, and tangy flavors in the marinade.

SERVES 4 AS PART OF A MULTI-COURSE MEAL
PREPARATION TIME: 10 MINUTES + MARINATING TIME
COOKING TIME: 30 MINUTES

1 lb (500 g) pork tenderloin
Sweet Thai Chili Sauce (page 24) or store-bought for dipping

BBQ MARINADE
4 garlic cloves, minced
2 tablespoons finely chopped fresh coriander leaves (cilantro)
2 tablespoons finely chopped Thai or Italian basil
1½ teaspoons Asian chili-garlic sauce, preferably sambal oelek
½ teaspoon white pepper
2 tablespoons palm or brown sugar
2 tablespoons honey
2 tablespoons oyster sauce
2 tablespoons fish sauce (nam pla)
1 tablespoon dark sesame oil
2 tablespoons freshly squeezed lime juice

1 BBQ Marinade: In a small bowl, whisk together the garlic, fresh coriander leaves, basil, chili-garlic sauce, pepper, palm sugar, honey, oyster sauce, fish sauce, sesame oil, and lime juice. Place pork tenderloin in a large sealable plastic bag and marinate for 6–8 hours (up to overnight) in the refrigerator.
2 Preheat oven to 350°F (175°C). Remove the pork from the bag and discard the marinade. Place the pork in a roasting pan and roast in the oven for 30 minutes or until the internal temperature reaches 135°F (57°C) to 140°F (60°C).
3 When pork has reached desired temperature, remove and let it sit on the cutting board for five minutes. Slice thinly and serve with a Sweet Thai Chili Sauce.

COOK'S NOTE: Use leftover slices for Thai BBQ Sliders drizzled with Sweet Thai Chili Sauce. They make a quick and delicious lunch.

Thai BBQ Pork

Stir-fried Pork with Spicy Green Beans

A fantastic dish to make on a busy weeknight because it's so darn simple. Omit the chilis or choose a mild type if you're making this for young kids. The sauce is so yummy that your family won't even realize they're gobbling up veggies. My family could literally eat bowls of rice with just the sauce because it's that tasty.

**SERVES 2 AS A MAIN DISH WITH RICE OR 4 AS PART OF A
MULTI-COURSE MEAL**
PREPARATION TIME: 5 MINUTES + BLANCHING TIME
COOKING TIME: 15 MINUTES

1½ oz (55 g) yard-long beans or green beans, sliced
    thinly into ¼ in (6 mm) discs
2 tablespoons high-heat cooking oil
2 cloves garlic, minced
2 fresh hot red or green chilies, preferably Thai (de-
    seeded if you prefer less heat), finely sliced
¾ lb (350 g) ground pork
1 tablespoon fish sauce (nam pla)
2 tablespoons oyster sauce
1 teaspoon soy sauce
1 teaspoon palm or brown sugar

1 Cook the beans in boiling water until tender-crisp, about 5 minutes. Using a slotted spoon, transfer the beans to an ice bath until cool. Drain the beans and set aside.
2 Heat the oil in a wok or skillet over medium-high heat. Add the garlic and chilies, stir-fry until fragrant, about 30 seconds. Add the ground pork and stir-fry, breaking it up with the back of a wooden spoon, about 5–6 minutes or until no longer pink. Add the fish sauce, oyster sauce, soy sauce, and palm sugar, stir-fry for 3 minutes. Add the green beans and stir-fry for 1 minute. Dish out and serve immediately with jasmine rice.

Shaking Beef

The northeastern Thai province of Issan has a large Vietnamese population and restaurants throughout the region serve this popular dish. It's called "shaking" because you don't stir-fry the beef, you merely shake the pan. Succulent filet mignon melts in your mouth as a result of the flavorful marinade and browning over high heat. Shaking is required, a shimmy is optional.

SERVES 4 AS PART OF A MULTI-COURSE MEAL
PREPARATION TIME: 15 MINUTES + MARINATING TIME
COOKING TIME: 4 MINUTES

10 oz (330 g) filet mignon, cut into 1 in (2.5 cm) cubes
1 tablespoon high-heat cooking oil

MARINADE
2 teaspoons fish sauce (nam pla)
½ tablespoon oyster sauce
2 garlic cloves, minced
1 teaspoon palm or brown sugar
½ teaspoon freshly ground black pepper
1 tablespoon vegetable or canola oil

DRESSING
2 tablespoons rice or white vinegar
1 tablespoon olive or canola oil
1 tablespoons palm or brown sugar
1 tablespoon cooking sherry
2 teaspoons fish sauce (nam pla)

SALAD
½ cup (58 g) thinly sliced white onion
8 cherry or grape tomatoes, halved
2 cups (60 g) bite-sized pieces of watercress or spinach, stemmed and washed

DIPPING SAUCE
1 tablespoon freshly squeezed lime juice
½ teaspoon salt
¼ teaspoon freshly ground black pepper

1 Marinade: In a large bowl, whisk together the fish sauce, oyster sauce, garlic, palm sugar, pepper, and oil. Add the beef and toss to coat. Let sit for 20 minutes at room temperature (or up to overnight in the refrigerator).
2 Dressing: Whisk together the vinegar, oil, sugar, sherry, and fish sauce in a small bowl. Set aside.
3 Heat the 1 tablespoon oil in the wok or skillet over high heat. Add the beef and let it sear without turning for a minute or two to get a good browning. "Shake" the skillet to turn the meat and let the other side cook the same way. Remove from heat and transfer with a slotted spoon to a plate.
4 Salad: Toss the Salad ingredients with the Dressing. Transfer to a serving platter. Place the beef on top. In a small bowl, combine the ingredients of the Dipping Sauce. Serve immediately with jasmine rice.

Beef with Ginger and Black Mushrooms

This dish is inspired by a visit to Ko Khun Beef restaurant in Bangkok. Their slogan is "Heaven is for Beef Lovers," because their quality and selection of beef is out of this world! Always cut beef across the grain to ensure the most tender result. You can substitute dried black mushrooms with dried shiitake mushrooms if you wish.

SERVES 2 AS A MAIN DISH WITH RICE OR 4 AS PART OF A MULTI-COURSE MEAL
PREPARATION TIME: 10 MINUTES
COOKING TIME: 8 MINUTES

8 medium, dried black mushrooms
10 oz (330 g) beef tenderloin or top sirloin, sliced diagonally across the grain in ¼ in (6 mm) slices
½ teaspoon all-purpose cornstarch
¼ teaspoon white pepper
1 teaspoon + 2 tablespoons high-heat cooking oil, divided
2 teaspoons soy sauce, divided
1 garlic clove, minced
1 tablespoon minced galangal or fresh ginger
1 fresh hot red or green chili, preferably Thai (deseeded if you prefer less heat), finely sliced
2 teaspoons fish sauce (nam pla)
1 teaspoon oyster sauce
1 teaspoon palm or brown sugar
Thai or Italian basil leaves, cut into thin shreds/threads for garnish

1 Soak the mushrooms in warm water until soft, about 30 minutes. Rinse in warm water and drain. Remove and discard stems and cut the caps in ½-inch (1.25 cm) pieces. Set aside

2 Toss the beef with the all-purpose cornstarch, pepper, 1 teaspoon oil, and 1 teaspoon soy sauce. Cover for 10 minutes at room temperature.

3 Heat 1 tablespoon of the oil in a wok or skillet over medium-high heat. Add the beef and stir-fry until the beef is brown, about 3 minutes. Remove the beef from the pan and set aside.

4 Heat the remaining oil in the wok or skillet over medium-high heat. Add the garlic, galangal, and chili to the wok or skillet and stir-fry until fragrant, about 30 seconds. Add the reserved beef, reserved mushrooms, fish sauce, oyster sauce, palm sugar, and remaining 1 teaspoon soy sauce. Garnish with basil leaves. Serve immediately with jasmine rice.

Panaeng Beef in Red Curry Peanut Sauce

Panaeng refers to a beautiful island on the west coast of Malaysia where this curry originated. Thai red curry and Penaeng curry are quite similar but Panaeng curry tends to be milder and thicker as it's fried in coconut cream as opposed to being boiled in coconut milk. The savory spices in the Penaeng curry paste are a wonderful complement to beef. I like to use beef tenderloin in this dish for extra tender results.

SERVES 6 AS A MAIN DISH WITH RICE AS PART OF A MULTI-COURSE MEAL
PREPARATION TIME: 10 MINUTES
COOKING TIME: 20 MINUTES

2 cups (500 ml) coconut milk
1 small carrot, sliced on a ¼ in (6 mm) diagonal
2 tablespoons Panaeng curry paste or thick red curry paste
1 fresh hot red or green chili, preferably Thai (deseeded if you prefer less heat), finely sliced
10 oz (330 g) beef tenderloin, rib eye or top sirloin, thinly sliced across grain

½ cup (50 g) sugar snap peas, trimmed and cut diagonally in ½ in (1.25 cm) pieces
2 tablespoons fish sauce (nam pla)
2 kaffir lime leaves, cut in half (optional)
¼ cup (37 g) canned sliced bamboo shoots, rinsed and drained
1 tablespoon chunky peanut butter
1 teaspoon palm or brown sugar
½ cup (10 g) fresh Thai or Italian basil leaves plus more for garnish

Bring ½ of the coconut milk and carrots to a medium boil in a wok or large skillet over medium-high heat. Cook for 3–4 minutes, stirring continuously. Add the panaeng curry paste and cook for 1–2 minutes, stirring until blended. Add the beef, sugar snap peas, and remaining coconut milk, bring to a boil. Reduce heat to medium-low and add the fish sauce, lime leaves (if using), bamboo shoots, peanut butter, palm sugar, and basil leaves. Stir to combine. Simmer for 4–5 minutes. Dish out and serve immediately with jasmine rice.

Chiang Mai Pork Curry

Chiang Mai Pork Curry is a popular dish throughout Northern Thailand with Burmese origins. I learned how to make this dish while attending the Chiang Mai Cookery School. It's traditionally made with water, but I used chicken stock for a more robust flavor. This dish simmers for an hour and is more stew-like than most Thai curries.

SERVES 4 AS A MAIN DISH WITH RICE AS PART OF A MULTI-COURSE MEAL
PREPARATION TIME: 20 MINUTES
COOKING TIME: 12 MINUTES

10 oz (330 g) pork tenderloin, cut into cubes
½ teaspoon all-purpose cornstarch
1 teaspoon soy sauce
¼ teaspoon white pepper
2 tablespoons high-heat cooking oil, divided
2 garlic cloves, minced
1 tablespoon minced galangal or fresh ginger
1 small shallot, finely sliced
1 tablespoon thick red curry paste
2 tablespoons tamarind water (1 teaspoon tamarind concentrate mixed with 2 tablespoons hot water)
2½ cups (625 ml) Basic Chicken Stock (page 26) or store-bought
2 teaspoons fish sauce (nam pla)
2 teaspoons palm or brown sugar
Crushed roasted peanuts for garnish
Finely chopped fresh coriander leaves (cilantro) for garnish

1 Toss the pork with the all-purpose cornstarch, soy sauce, and pepper. Cover and refrigerate for 10 minutes.
2 Heat ½ of the oil in a wok or skillet over medium-high heat. Add the pork and stir-fry until it changes color, about 2 minutes. Remove the pork from pan and set aside. Wash and thoroughly dry the wok or skillet.
3 Heat the remaining oil in the wok or skillet over medium-high heat. Add the garlic, galangal, and shallots to the wok or skillet and stir-fry until fragrant, about 30 seconds. Reduce heat to medium. Add the curry paste and stir-fry, stirring to break it up, about 1 minute. Add the reserved pork, tamarind water, chicken stock, fish sauce, and palm sugar. Bring to a gentle boil and reduce heat to medium-low. Cover and simmer for 1 hour. Garnish with peanuts and fresh coriander leaves. Dish out and serve immediately with jasmine rice.

Crying Tiger Lamb

Hey, cry baby! It's okay to cry especially when you're enjoying this spicy dish which got its name because it's so hot it'll make a tiger howl. It's traditionally made with beef but I decided to try this version with lamb. You could easily swap out the lamb chops with some flank steak or filet mignon if you're craving steak.

SERVES 6 AS A MAIN DISH AS PART OF A MULTI-COURSE MEAL
PREPARATION TIME: 5 MINUTES + MARINATING TIME
COOKING TIME: 10 MINUTES

4 lamb loin chops
½ cup (14 g) finely chopped fresh coriander leaves (cilantro) leaves

MARINADE
1 tablespoon oil
2 tablespoons fish sauce (nam pla)
1 tablespoon soy sauce
1 tablespoon palm or brown sugar
3 cloves garlic, minced
1 teaspoon freshly ground black pepper

SAUCE
2 tablespoons fish sauce (nam pla)
2 tablespoons freshly squeezed lime juice
1 teaspoon sugar
3 fresh hot red or green chilies, preferably Thai (deseeded if you prefer less heat), finely sliced
1 tablespoon finely chopped shallots

1 Make the Marinade: Whisk together the oil, fish sauce, soy sauce, palm sugar, garlic, and pepper. Place the lamb loins in a large sealable plastic bag and pour Marinade over lamb. Place in refrigerator for at least 2 hours (and up to 8 hours).
2 Sauce: Whisk the fish sauce, lime juice, sugar, chilies, and shallots in a small bowl until combined.
3 Heat a grill to medium-high and brush with oil. Grill the lamb loins over medium high heat until desired doneness is reached, about 5 minutes per side for medium rare. Let rest for 5 minutes. Slice thinly and arrange on a serving platter. Drizzle Sauce on top and garnish with fresh coriander leaves before serving. Serve immediately with jasmine rice.

COOK'S NOTE: Reduce the amount of chilies if you'd prefer a slight whimper over a howl.

Crying Tiger Lamb

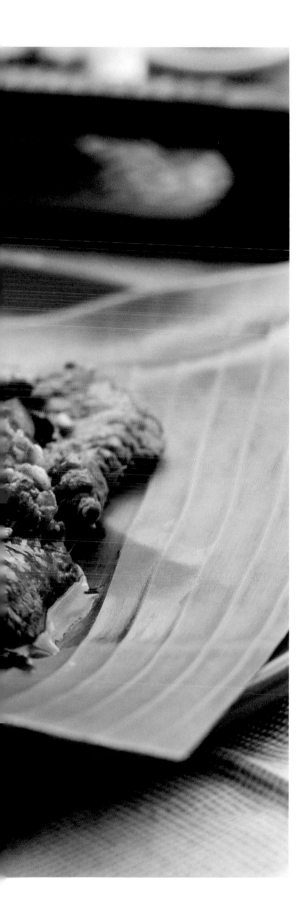

Beef with Red Chili Paste and Lime Leaves

My house fills with the incredible aroma of kaffir lime leaves and roasted red chili paste when I make this dish. My friend Gary Arabia of Global Cuisine was kind of enough to give me some of his kaffir lime seeds so I'm excited to see our own tree sprouting soon. Gary's cuisine and masterful use of kaffir lime leaves inspired me to create this simple, yet intensely flavored dish.

SERVES 2 AS A MAIN DISH WITH RICE OR 4 AS PART OF A MULTI-COURSE MEAL
PREPARATION TIME: 20 MINUTES
COOKING TIME: 12 MINUTES

10 oz (330 g) beef tenderloin or top sirloin, sliced diagonally across the grain in ¼ in (6 mm) slices
½ teaspoon all-purpose cornstarch
¼ teaspoon white pepper
1 teaspoon + 2 tablespoons high-heat cooking oil, divided
1 teaspoon soy sauce
1 garlic clove, minced
1 small shallot, finely sliced
1 fresh hot red or green chili, preferably Thai (deseeded if you prefer less heat), finely sliced
1 small red bell pepper, thinly sliced
1 tablespoon freshly squeezed lime juice
1 tablespoon fish sauce (nam pla)
1 tablespoon Roasted Red Chili Paste (page 23) or store-bought, (nam pla, optional)
2 kaffir lime leaves, cut into thin strips (optional)
2 teaspoons palm or brown sugar
¾ cup (15 g) fresh Thai or Italian basil leaves

1 Toss the beef with the all-purpose cornstarch, pepper, 1 teaspoon oil, and soy sauce. Cover for 10 minutes at room temperature.
2 Heat ½ of the oil in a wok or skillet over medium-high heat. Add the beef and stir-fry until it's brown, about 3 minutes. Remove the beef from the pan and set aside. Wash and thoroughly dry the wok or skillet.
3 Heat the remaining oil in the wok or skillet over medium-high heat. Add the garlic, shallots, and chili to the wok or skillet and stir-fry until fragrant, about 1 minute. Add the red pepper and stir-fry for 1 minute. Add the reserved beef, lime juice, fish sauce, roasted red chili paste (if using), kaffir lime leaves (if using), and palm sugar; stir-fry for 1–2 minutes or until the beef is cooked through. Add the basil leaves and stir-fry for about 30 seconds or until wilted. Dish out and serve immediately with jasmine rice.

CHAPTER SIX

Seafood

We went crazy for all the amazing seafood dishes we enjoyed throughout Thailand on our honeymoon. My favorite memory was going to an outdoor seafood market where we picked out some clams. After ringing us up, the man who ran the stall pointed us to the restaurant next door. The chef took our bag and whipped up a fantastic Clams with Roasted Chili Basil Sauce (which I've recreated on page 93) right before our eyes. You can't get fresher than that!

Seafood is a large part of the Thai diet as fish and shellfish caught from the Mekong River, as well as the ocean and lakes has been an abundant and cheap source of food for Southeast Asians for centuries. Battered, stir-fried, grilled, roasted, and put in soups and salads, Thai seafood dishes are limitless, colorful, bold, and unpredictable.

Preparing a whole fish is a grand gesture in Asian cuisine and is served with pride. I've included a couple of whole fish recipes such as Whole Catfish in Coriander-Chili Sauce (page 101) that is roasted until tender and flaky and topped with a bright, zesty, and colorful sauce. There's also preparations using fish filets for convenience such as Grilled Fresh Salmon with Green Curry Sauce (page 90), which is super easy and healthy. Grilled Halibut in a Mango Coconut Sauce (page 91) is perfect for a summer night BBQ. Shrimp is a great thing to keep in your freezer because you can quickly defrost it and make a Thai stir-fry within minutes like Shrimp, Lemongrass, and Basil (page 96) or the quick-simmered Thai Green Curry with Prawns (page 92).

Grilled Fresh Salmon with Green Curry Sauce

Some of my friends have become flexitarians, meaning "I'm mostly vegetarian, but sometimes eat fish," that I always serve a fish or seafood dish when entertaining. Green curry paste's green hue comes green chilies as well as basil, fresh coriander leaves (cilantro), and kaffir lime leaves. This simple melt-in-your-mouth salmon dish is light and delicious but full of flavor.

SERVES 2 AS A MAIN DISH WITH RICE OR 4 AS PART OF A MULTI-COURSE MEAL
PREPARATION TIME: 10 MINUTES + MARINATING TIME
COOKING TIME: 30 MINUTES

Two 5 oz (150 g) fresh salmon fillets or steaks

MARINADE
1 teaspoon minced galangal or fresh ginger
2 tablespoons fish sauce (nam pla)
1 tablespoon soy sauce
1 tablespoon palm or brown sugar
1 tablespoon freshly squeezed lime juice

GREEN CURRY SAUCE
1 tablespoon high-heat cooking oil
½ tablespoon green curry paste
½ cup (125 ml) coconut milk
4 tablespoons Basic Chicken Stock (page 26) or store-bought
1 tablespoon fish sauce (nam pla)
1 teaspoon palm or brown sugar
2 teaspoons freshly squeezed lime juice
1 tablespoon finely chopped fresh Thai or Italian basil

1 Marinade: In a small bowl, whisk together the galangal, fish sauce, soy sauce, palm sugar, and lime juice. Place the salmon in a large sealable plastic bag. Pour the Marinade over the salmon and marinate for 1–2 hours in the refrigerator.
2 Green Curry Sauce: Heat oil in small saucepan over medium heat. Add the curry paste, stirring to break up the paste, about 1 minute. Add the coconut milk, chicken stock, fish sauce, and palm sugar, bring to a gentle boil for 2–3 minutes. Reduce the heat to medium-low and simmer for 5 minutes. Stir in the lime juice and basil. Keep warm.
3 Heat a grill to medium and brush with oil. Place the salmon on a grill and cook for 6–8 minutes per side, or until the fish flakes easily with a fork. Transfer the salmon to a serving platter and spoon ½ of the Green Curry Sauce over it before serving. Serve immediately with jasmine rice with the remaining curry sauce in a small serving bowl.

Grilled Fresh Salmon with Green Curry Sauce

Grilled Halibut in a Mango Coconut Sauce

Breezy, light, and healthy, this recipe is the perfect dish to grill on a warm summer night paired with a glass of sauvignon blanc. The mango coconut sauce is so delicious I love to drizzle it on shrimp, roast chicken and any type of grilled fish. I usually make a double or triple batch and freeze the rest because it's so great to have on hand.

SERVES 2 AS A MAIN DISH WITH RICE OR 4 AS PART OF A MULTI-COURSE MEAL
PREPARATION TIME: 15 MINUTES + MARINATING TIME
COOKING TIME: 20 MINUTES

Two 6 oz (175 g) halibut fillets

MARINADE
1 tablespoon fish sauce (nam pla)
2 teaspoons oyster sauce
2 teaspoons palm or brown sugar
3 garlic cloves, minced
2 teaspoons freshly squeezed lime juice
1 fresh hot red or green chili, preferably Thai (deseeded if you prefer less heat), finely sliced

SAUCE
2 tablespoons unsalted butter
2 garlic cloves, minced
1 tablespoon finely chopped green onions (white and green parts)
1 tablespoon finely chopped fresh coriander leaves (cilantro)
1 tablespoon minced galangal or fresh ginger
1 tablespoon minced lemongrass
½ teaspoon salt
¼ cup (42 g) diced fresh mango, puréed in a blender
2 tablespoons honey
1 cup (250 ml) coconut milk
2 teaspoons Asian chili sauce, preferably Sriracha

1 Marinade: In a small bowl, whisk together the fish sauce, oyster sauce, palm sugar, garlic, lime juice, and chili. Place the halibut steaks in a large sealable plastic bag. Pour the Marinade over the halibut and marinate for 1–2 hours in the refrigerator.

2 Sauce: In a medium saucepan, melt the butter over medium heat. Add the garlic, green onions, fresh coriander leaves, galangal, and lemongrass. Stir-fry until the garlic is fragrant, about 30 seconds. Add salt, puréed mango, and honey, stir-fry for 2–3 minutes. Add the coconut milk and chili sauce, and simmer, stirring occasionally, for about 5 minutes. Remove from the heat. Set aside, covered.

3 Heat a grill to medium and brush with oil. Place the halibut on the grill and cook for 3–4 minutes per side, or until the fish flakes easily with a fork. Transfer the halibut to a serving platter and spoon half of the Sauce over the fish before serving. Serve the remaining Sauce in a small bowl for dipping.

COOK'S NOTE: If mangos aren't in season, you can use frozen mango chunks. I like Trader Joe's which are frozen at the peak of freshness and perfectly ripe.

Thai Green Curry with Prawns

This soul satisfying and easy one-pot meal can be made in minutes. This is an excellent green curry sauce base which you can use for any type of seafood dish.

SERVES 6 AS A MAIN DISH WITH RICE AS PART OF A MULTI-COURSE MEAL
PREPARATION TIME: 10 MINUTES
COOKING TIME: 15 MINUTES

1 tablespoon high-heat cooking oil
4 tablespoons finely chopped green onion (white part only)
1 garlic clove, minced
1 small shallot, finely sliced
1 fresh hot red or green chili, preferably Thai (deseeded if you prefer less heat), finely sliced
4 tablespoons minced lemongrass
1 tablespoon green curry paste
1 cup (250 ml) coconut milk
½ cup (125 ml) Basic Chicken Stock (page 26) or store-bought
1 tablespoon fish sauce (nam pla)
3 kaffir lime leaves, torn in half (optional)
¼ teaspoon freshly ground black pepper
1 teaspoon palm or brown sugar
6 cherry or grape tomatoes, quartered
10 oz (330 g) medium-sized shrimp, peeled and deveined
Finely chopped fresh coriander leaves (cilantro) for garnish
Lime wedges

1 Heat oil in a medium saucepan over medium-high heat. Add the green onion, garlic, shallots, chili, lemongrass, and stir-fry until fragrant, about 1 minute.
2 Reduce heat to medium. Add the green curry paste and stir-fry, stirring to break it up, about 1 more minute. Add coconut milk, chicken stock, fish sauce, kaffir lime leaves (if using), pepper, and palm sugar; bring to a gentle boil. Add tomatoes and cook for 2 minutes. Reduce heat to medium-low and bring to a simmer. Add shrimp and simmer until cooked through, about 3 minutes. Dish out and serve with jasmine rice. Garnish with fresh coriander leaves and lime wedges on the side.

Clams with Roasted Chili Basil Sauce

Koh Samui is known for its seafood and I remember lingering over these flavorful clams with a huge pitcher of Thai beer after a glorious day at the beach. I was amazed at how easy it was to recreate this dish at home and I love making it for guests because dinner is on the table in a matter of minutes.

Clams are purchased alive and must be kept alive. It's best to purchase them right before cooking but if you need to buy them in advance they should be kept cool and moist on ice in the refrigerator.

SERVES 4 AS PART OF A MULTI-COURSE MEAL
PREPARATION TIME: 10 MINUTES + CLAM CLEANING TIME
COOKING TIME: 10 MINUTES

2 dozen manila, littleneck or cherrystone clams, debearded and scrubbed clean
2 tablespoons high-heat cooking oil, divided
6 garlic cloves, minced
1 small shallot, finely sliced
2 fresh hot red or green chilies, preferably Thai (deseeded if you prefer less heat), sliced lengthwise
1 tablespoon Roasted Red Chili Paste (page 23) or store-bought
2 teaspoons palm or brown sugar
2 tablespoons Basic Fish Stock (page 27) or store-bought clam juice or water
2 teaspoons fish sauce (nam pla)
1 cup (20 g) fresh Thai or Italian basil leaves

1 Heat half of the oil in the wok or skillet over medium-high heat. Add the garlic, shallots, and chilies, stir-fry until fragrant, about 30 seconds. Add the Roasted Red Chili Paste and stir-fry, stirring to break it up, about 1 minute.
2 Add the remaining oil and the clams and stir-fry 3–4 minutes, or until the shells just begin to open. Add the palm sugar, fish stock, and fish sauce. Stir-fry for 1 minute. Add the basil leaves and stir-fry for 30 seconds or until the basil wilts. Dish out and serve with jasmine rice.

COOK'S NOTE: Just before cooking, scrub them with a stiff brush under cool running water and trim off beards if they have them. If any of them are open, tap the shell. If they don't close tightly, discard them. If any don't open when cooked, discard them.

Clams with Roasted Chili Basil Sauce

Pan Seared Scallops on Coconut Rice

My late mother always taught me to serve scallops when I didn't know what to make for a dinner party because they're easy to make but always make your friends feel special. If you're looking for a simple, yet elegant dish to serve at your next dinner party, this is it. Impress your dinner guests or treat your family with these scallops which are sweet, mild, and tender, basking in a sublime sauce over fragrant coconut rice.

SERVES 6 AS PART OF A MULTI-COURSE MEAL
PREPARATION TIME: 15 MINUTES
COOKING TIME: 30 MINUTES

½ cup (112 g) uncooked jasmine rice
1 cup (250 ml) coconut milk
½ cup (125 ml) water
8–10 large scallops
1 teaspoon + 1 tablespoon high-heat cooking oil, divided
Salt and pepper to taste
Finely chopped fresh coriander leaves (cilantro) for garnish
Lime wedges

SAUCE
1 garlic clove, minced
2 teaspoons minced galangal or fresh ginger
4 tablespoons finely chopped green onions (white part only)
2 teaspoons yellow curry paste or 2 teaspoons thick red curry paste mixed with 1 teaspoon curry powder
½ cup (46 g) finely chopped red pepper
1 cup (250 ml) coconut milk
½ cup (125 ml) Basic Chicken Stock (page 26) or store-bought
1 teaspoon fish sauce (nam pla)
½ teaspoon soy sauce
1 teaspoon palm or brown sugar

1 Wash the rice in cool water by rubbing it gently between your fingers; drain. Repeat washing the rice until the water is clear, 5 or 6 times; drain. In a medium, heavy-bottomed pot with a tight-fitting lid, combine ¾ cups (185 ml) water and the rice. Bring to a boil over high heat. As soon as the water is boiling, lower the heat to a simmer and cover. Cook at a gentle simmer until the water is completely absorbed and the rice is tender, about 12 minutes. Remove from the heat and let sit for 5 minutes with the lid on.
2 Rinse the scallops and pat dry with paper towels. With your fingers, peel away the small tab of tough connective tissue on the side of each scallop. Heat 1 teaspoon of the oil in a skillet over high heat. Sear the scallops until opaque in color and seared on edges to a golden brown color, about 2 minutes per side. Salt and pepper to taste. Remove from heat and set aside.
3 Sauce: Heat the remaining 1 tablespoon oil in a medium saucepan over medium-high heat. Add the garlic, galangal, and onions and stir-fry until fragrant, about 1 minute. Reduce heat to medium. Add 2 teaspoons yellow curry paste or 2 teaspoons thick red curry paste mixed with 1 teaspoon curry powder and stir-fry, stirring to break it up, about 1 minute. Add the red pepper and cook for 1 minute. Add the coconut milk, chicken stock, fish sauce, soy sauce, and

palm sugar, bring to a gentle boil. Reduce heat to medium-low and bring to a simmer for 4–5 minutes. Keep warm until ready to serve.
4 Fluff the jasmine rice with a rice paddle or fork and scoop onto a serving platter. Slightly flatten rice and place scallops on top and spoon sauce over before serving. Garnish with fresh coriander leaves and serve with lime wedges on the side.

COOK'S NOTE: When buying scallops, make sure to ask for "dry" scallops. If they're not "dry" they were previously frozen and possibly treated to a phosphate preservative which leaves a funny aftertaste when they're cooked.

Shrimp, Lemongrass, and Basil

I love the woodsy lemony notes in this dish from the lemongrass which pairs so well with shrimp. I like to make this dish when we have last minute guests because most of the ingredients are in my pantry and I usually have frozen shrimp in my freezer.

**SERVES 2 AS A MAIN DISH WITH RICE OR 4
AS PART OF A MULTI-COURSE MEAL
PREPARATION TIME: 20 MINUTES
COOKING TIME: 10 MINUTES**

10 oz (330 g) medium-sized shrimp, peeled and deveined
½ teaspoon dark sesame oil
½ teaspoon all-purpose cornstarch
Pinch of white pepper
2 tablespoons high-heat cooking oil, divided
4 tablespoons minced lemongrass
1 clove garlic, minced
1 small shallot, thinly sliced

1 fresh hot red or green chili, preferably Thai (deseeded if you prefer less heat), finely sliced
2 kaffir lime leaves, finely sliced (optional)
1 teaspoon soy sauce
2 teaspoons fish sauce (nam pla)
1½ teaspoons sugar
1 cup (20 g) fresh Thai or Italian basil leaves

1 Toss the shrimp with the sesame oil, all-purpose cornstarch, and pepper in a small bowl. Cover and refrigerate for 10 minutes.
2 Heat ½ of the oil in a wok or skillet over medium-high heat. Add the shrimp and stir-fry until the shrimp turns pink. Remove the shrimp from the pan and set aside. Wash and thoroughly dry the wok or skillet.
3 Heat the remaining oil in the wok or skillet over medium-high heat. Add the lemongrass, garlic, shallots and chilies, stir-fry until fragrant, about 1 minute. Add the reserved shrimp, kaffir lime leaves (if using), soy sauce, fish sauce, and sugar; stir-fry for 2 minutes or until shrimp is cooked through. Add the basil leaves and stir-fry for about 30 seconds or until basil is wilted. Dish out and serve immediately with jasmine rice.

Seafood Feast with Basil and Chilies

This recipe is inspired by a dish we had at the popular Seafood Market and Restaurant in Bangkok. My sister Jeanie lives on Bainbridge Island, Washington and she helped me recreate this dish after a seafood shopping spree at Central Market, famous for its gorgeous assortment of fish and shellfish.

SERVES 2 AS A MAIN DISH WITH RICE OR 4 AS PART OF A MULTI-COURSE MEAL
PREPARATION TIME: 20 MINUTES
COOKING TIME: 18 MINUTES

6 medium-sized shrimp, peeled and deveined
4 oz (100 g) bay scallops
4 oz (100 g) boneless fish fillet (such as sole), cut into 1 x 1.5 in (2.5 x 3.75 cm) pieces
½ teaspoon dark sesame oil
½ teaspoon all-purpose cornstarch
¼ teaspoon white pepper
3 tablespoons high-heat cooking oil, divided
4 dried Thai chilies or Chiles de Arbol
2 garlic cloves, minced
1 tablespoon minced galangal or fresh ginger
½ small white onion, cut into wedges
1½ teaspoons Roasted Red Chili Paste (page 23) or store-bought (nam prik pao, optional)
⅓ cup (80 ml) Basic Chicken Stock (page 26) or store-bought
2 teaspoons fish sauce (nam pla)
2 teaspoons soy sauce
1½ teaspoons sugar
½ cup (10 g) fresh Thai or Italian basil leaves

1 Toss the shrimp, scallops, and fish with the sesame oil, all-purpose cornstarch, salt, and pepper in a medium bowl. Cover and refrigerate for 10 minutes.

2 Heat 2 tablespoons of the oil in a wok or skillet over medium-high heat. Add the shrimp, scallops, and fish, stir-fry until the shrimp turns pink. Remove from the pan and set aside. Wash and thoroughly dry the wok or skillet.

3 Heat the remaining 1 tablespoon of oil in the wok or skillet over medium-high heat. Add the chilies and stir-fry for 1 minute. Remove the chilies with a slotted spoon and set aside. Add the garlic, galangal, and onion to the wok or skillet and stir-fry until te garlic is fragrant and onion is translucent, about 1 minute. Add the chili paste (if using) and stir-fry, stirring to break it up, about 1 minute.

4 Add the chicken stock, fish sauce, soy sauce, and sugar. Stir until combined and simmer for 3 minutes. Lower the heat to medium, add the reserved seafood and cook until the sauce starts to thicken, about 4–5 minutes. Add the basil leaves and stir-fry for 30 seconds or until the basil wilts. Dish out and serve immediately with jasmine rice.

How to Make Fragrant Coconut Fish in Banana Leaves

1 Prepare the fish for marinating by sprinkling with salt and pepper.

4 Fold in the other sides of the large rectangle, then fold in the remaiing two sides.

2 Pour the marinade over the fish and toss to coat evenly.

5 Once folded, it should resemble a packet.

3 Place 3–4 pieces of fish on each smaller rectangle. Fold one side of the large rectangle over the fish.

6 Secure the packet firmly with a toothpick.

Fragrant Coconut Fish in Banana Leaves

I ask my friend, Stacy, to come cook this dish with me because she's so meticulous about wrapping birthday presents, plus she's an amazing cook. Although it may seem intimidating to make this dish, it's not hard at all. You can use foil or parchment paper if you don't have banana leaves although they make the most beautiful presentation. Slathered in fragrant coconut sauce, this fish is amazingly tender, super healthy and will impress your guests.

SERVES 4 AS PART OF A MULTI-COURSE MEAL
**PREPARATION TIME: 30 MINUTES + MARINAT-
 ING TIME**
COOKING TIME: 20 MINUTES

1 lb (500 g) skinless sea bass, flounder
 or tilapia fillets, cut into 2 in (5 cm)
 pieces
Salt and black pepper
8 banana leaves (see tips, at left)
Hot water
8 toothpicks

MARINADE
3 kaffir lime leaves, finely sliced (optional)
4 tablespoons minced lemongrass
2 cloves garlic, smashed
1 small shallot
1 fresh hot red or green chili, preferably Thai (deseeded if you prefer less
 heat), finely sliced
½ cup (10 g) coarsely chopped fresh
 basil
1 tablespoon minced galangal or fresh
 ginger
2 teaspoons ground coriander
½ teaspoon ground turmeric
½ teaspoon palm or brown sugar
¼ cup (65 ml) coconut milk
2 tablespoons fish sauce (nam
 pla)
1 tablespoon freshly squeezed lime
 juice
Lime wedges

1 Place the fish on a large baking sheet and sprinkle it evenly with salt and pepper.
2 Marinade: In a food processor, combine the kaffir lime leaves (if using), lemongrass, garlic, shallot, chili, basil, galangal, coriander, turmeric, palm sugar, coconut milk, fish sauce, and lime juice and purée until smooth.
3 Pour the Marinade over the fish, tossing to coat evenly. Cover and refrigerate for 15 minutes.
4 Meanwhile, remove the ribs from the banana leaves and place the leaves in a large bowl of hot water for 1 minute to soften and avoid tearing. Cut the leaves into four 12 x 8-inch (27 x 20 cm) rectangles and four 6 x 3-inch (15 x 7.5 cm) rectangles. Place the large rectangles in front of you on a cutting board.
5 Using a slotted spoon, place 3–4 pieces of fish on each smaller rectangle. Fold the sides of the large rectangle up to form a packet and secure firmly with a toothpick, taking extra care that the Marinade doesn't leak. Continue until you have 4 packets. Discard the remaining Marinade.
6 Add 2 inches (5 cm) water to a large pot and bring to a rolling boil. Place the fish packets on a heat proof plate. Place the plate on a steaming rack or basket and steam for 20 minutes. Remove from the fish packets from the steamer and serve immediately with lime wedges and jasmine rice.

COOK'S NOTE: I recommend cutting one banana leaf according to directions and using it as a pattern to cut the remaining leaves.

Whole Crispy Seabass with Sweet Garlic-Chili Sauce

This dish makes for a beautiful presentation. I recommend using a round platter and positioning the fish in a yin-yang shape. Serving a whole fish is a grand gesture in Asian culture and the head of the fish should be pointed at the eldest sitting at the table as a sign of respect.

SERVES 4 AS PART OF A MULTI-COURSE MEAL
PREPARATION TIME: 10 MINUTES + MARINATING TIME
COOKING TIME: 25 MINUTES

2 whole sea bass or striped bass (about 1 pound each)
1½ teaspoons salt
1½ teaspoons dark sesame oil
Two ¼ in (6 mm) thick slices fresh ginger
⅓ cup (42 g) all-purpose cornstarch
Oil for frying

SAUCE
½ cup (125 ml) Sweet Thai Chili sauce (page 24) or store-bought
1 tablespoon fish sauce (nam pla)
1 teaspoon dark sesame oil
2 teaspoons soy sauce
4 tablespoons finely chopped fresh coriander leaves (cilantro)
½ teaspoon freshly ground black pepper
4 garlic cloves, minced
2 tablespoons freshly squeezed lime juice
2 tablespoons palm or brown sugar
2 fresh hot red or green chili, preferably Thai (deseeded if you prefer less heat), finely sliced
Fresh coriander leaves (cilantro) for garnish

1 Slash the fish crosswise 3 times on each side. Mix the salt and sesame oil and rub cavities and outsides of each fish with the mixture. Cover and refrigerate 1–2 hours.
2 Sauce: Whisk together the sweet Thai chili sauce, fish sauce, sesame oil, soy sauce, fresh coriander leaves, pepper, garlic, lime juice, palm sugar, and chilies in a small bowl. Transfer to a small saucepan and bring it to a low simmer. Keep warm.
3 Heat 2–3 inches (5–7.5 cm) of the oil in a wok to 350°F (175°C). Coat the fish with ⅓ cup cornstarch. Fry one fish until golden brown, turning once, about 8 minutes. Transfer it carefully onto a sheet pan. Keep the fish warm in 300°F (150°C) oven. Repeat the steps with the remaining fish.
4 Transfer both fish to a serving platter and spoon half of the Sauce on top before serving. Garnish with fresh coriander leaves. Serve immediately with jasmine rice and remaining Sauce in a small bowl for dipping.

Whole Catfish in Coriander Chili Sauce

Whole Catfish in Coriander Chili Sauce

My Thai friend, Tamalin, told me that Thai people never flip a whole fish after eating through one side. You're supposed to carefully remove the bones and continue eating from the same side as superstition says that flipping the fish will cause fishermen to flip their boats! All I know is that you'll flip after trying this incredibly moist and flavorful dish.

SERVES 4 AS PART OF A MULTI-COURSE MEAL
PREPARATION TIME: 10 MINUTES + MARINATING TIME
COOKING TIME: 30 MINUTES

One 2–3 lb (1 kg–1.5 kg) whole catfish, cleaned
   and gutted
Fresh coriander leaves (cilantro) for garnish

MARINADE
1 tablespoon minced galangal or fresh ginger
2 tablespoons fish sauce (nam pla)
2 tablespoons soy sauce
1 tablespoon palm or brown sugar
1 tablespoon freshly squeezed lime juice
4 lime slices
1 bunch fresh coriander leaves (cilantro), divided
1 bunch Thai or Italian basil leaves, divided

SAUCE
½ small white onion, finely chopped
2 tablespoons finely chopped fresh coriander
   leaves (cilantro)
2 teaspoons palm or brown sugar
1½ teaspoons Asian chili-garlic sauce, preferably
   sambal oelek
2 tablespoons freshly squeezed lime juice
1 tablespoon fish sauce (nam pla)
1 tablespoons toasted sesame oil
½ cup (46 g) red pepper, finely chopped

1 Marinade: Whisk together the galangal, fish sauce, soy sauce, palm sugar, and lime juice in a small bowl. Make 3 slits on both sides of catfish. Pour the Marinade all over the fish including the cavity and in slits. Stuff the cavity with ½ of the fresh coriander leaves, ½ of the basil and lime slices. Cover with plastic wrap and refrigerate for 1–2 hours.
2 Preheat oven to 350°F (175°C). Roast the catfish on a cookie sheet for about 30 minutes, or until the fish flakes easily.
3 Sauce: Whisk together the onion, fresh coriander leaves, palm sugar, chili-garlic sauce, lime juice, fish sauce, and sesame oil. Add the red pepper and stir to combine.
4 Transfer the catfish to a platter lined with the remaining fresh coriander and basil leaves; spoon the Sauce over the fish before serving. Garnish with fresh coriander leaves and serve immediately.

COOK'S NOTE: You can substitute with striped bass, tilapia or any whole fish of your liking.

CHAPTER SEVEN

Noodles and Rice

I have Thai noodle fever. Sipped, slurped, and twirled, noodles are a beloved part of Thai cuisine and come in all sorts of shapes and sizes. The array of Thai noodles is dizzying—egg noodles, cellophane noodles, fresh rice noodles, thin vermicelli noodles, dried rice noodles—it goes on and on. I've picked a handful of my Thai noodle favorites for this chapter. Just talking about it makes me want to whip some up right now! Since Thai noodles are made of either rice or mung beans, they're fantastic for most gluten-free diets.

The preparation of Thai noodles is just as diverse. My friends begged me to create a user-friendly, failproof Pad Thai recipe (page 106) and here it is. I was excited to include the legendary, palace dish Sweet and Tangy Thai Noodles (*Mee Krob*) (page 113), a layered, complex noodle dish of crispy noodles in a tangy, sweet and sour sauce. I am absolutely in love with the Glass Noodles with Crab recipe (page 109) generously given to me by wok star Chef Mohan from the popular Rock Sugar restaurant in Century City, CA.

And let's not forget about rice. Thai people greet each other by saying "Gin Khao," which literally translates to "have you eaten rice today?" This is a testament to the place of honor rice is given at the table by Thai people. Thais consider rice to be the center of any given meal with everything else serving as just an accompaniment. Like in China and other Asian cultures, rice and noodles are a huge part of everyday life. In fact, many Thai people eat fried rice for breakfast as well as throughout the day. Like most people who grew up in an Asian-American household, I start experiencing withdrawals if I go without rice for two days. On the third day, I start getting the shakes.

Turn to the Cooking Techniques and Tips (page 13) to learn how to make perfect steamed jasmine rice. I recommend you serve jasmine rice with almost all of the main dishes in this book. This chapter includes other classic Thai rice favorites including the ubiquitous and popular Pineapple Fried Rice (page 115), which I love because it's bursting with fresh pineapple and bold Thai flavors. There's also luxurious Crab Fried Rice (page 111) which will transport you to the beaches of Phuket.

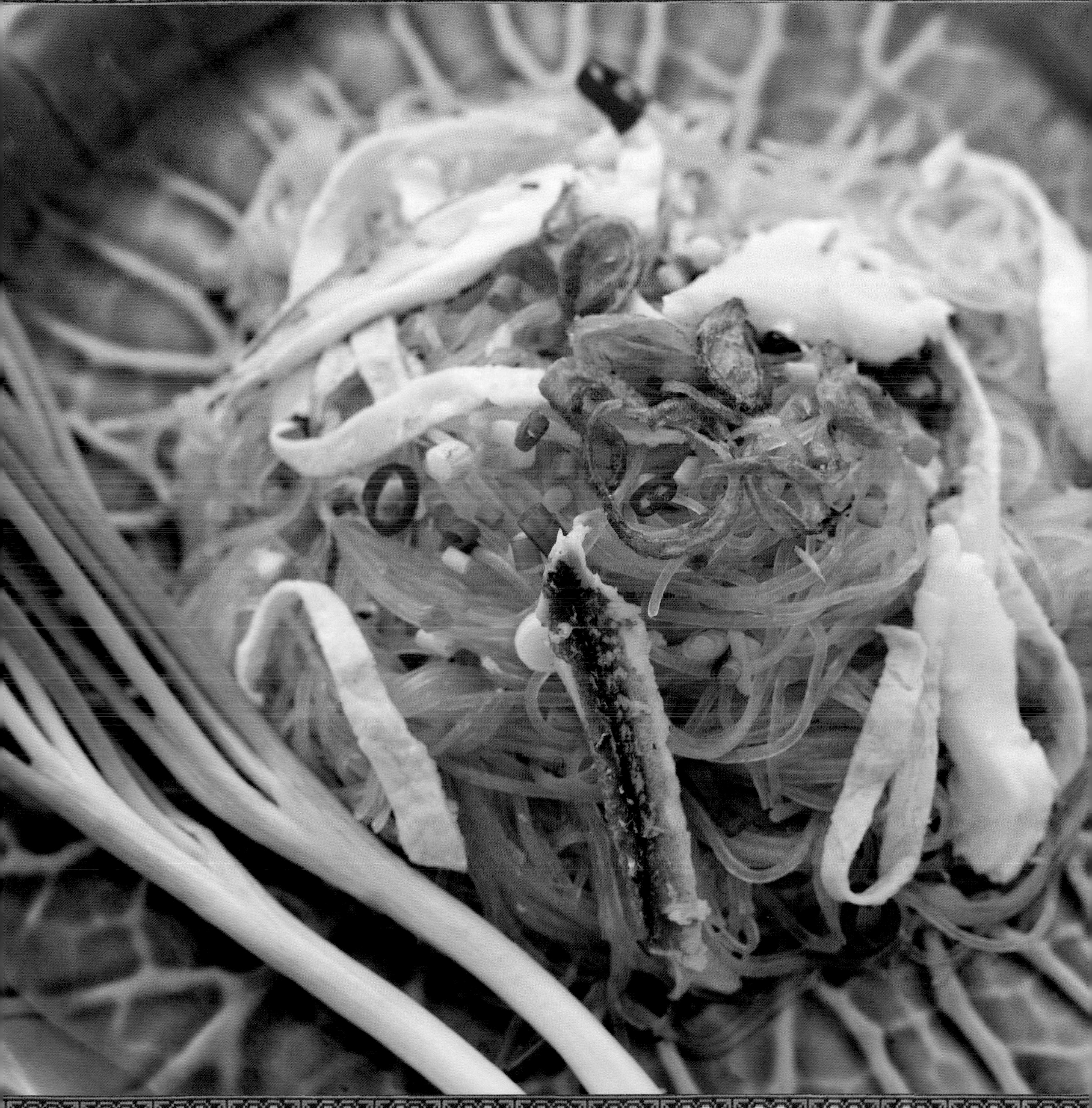

Thai Flat Noodles
(Seafood Rad Na)

Rad na are thick rice noodles covered in generous gravy which is very similar to a classic Chinese chow fun dish. This is a mild, stir-fry noodle dish which appeals to more conservative palates and young kids. Feel free to serve along with some Srircha if you wish. *Rad na* noodles can be found all over Thailand and is therefore considered a national dish.

**SERVES 3 AS A MAIN DISH OR 4–6 AS PART OF A
   MULTI-COURSE MEAL**
**PREPARATION TIME: 20 MINUTES + BLANCHING
   TIME**
COOKING TIME: 10 MINUTES

1½ lbs (740 g) fresh flat rice noodles
6 medium-sized shrimp, peeled and deveined
4 oz (100 g) cleaned calamari, cut into rings
4 oz (100 g) baby scallops
1 teaspoon all-purpose cornstarch
½ teaspoon dark sesame oil
Pinch of white pepper
6 oz (175 g) broccoli florets
2 tablespoons oil
1½ tablespoons dark soy sauce
2 garlic cloves, minced
1 tablespoon yellow bean paste (optional)
2½ cups (625 ml) Basic Chicken Stock
   (page 26) or store-bought
1 tablespoon oyster sauce
1 tablespoon fish sauce (nam pla)
1 tablespoon sugar
¼ cup (32 g) all-purpose cornstarch mixed
   with ½ cup (125 ml) water
Thinly sliced green onion for garnish
Fresh coriander leaves (cilantro) for
   garnish

Thai Flat Noodles

1 Loosen the flat noodles completely so they don't clump together.
2 Toss the shrimp, squid, and scallops with the all-purpose cornstarch, sesame oil, and pepper in a medium bowl. Cover and refrigerate for 10 minutes.
3 Bring a small saucepan of water to a boil. Add broccoli and boil for 1 minute or until tender-crisp. Using a slotted spoon, transfer the broccoli to a bowl of ice water and let it cool completely. Drain, and set aside.
4 Heat ½ of the oil in a wok or skillet over medium-high heat. Add the rice noodles and soy sauce and stir-fry until the noodles are coated well, about 1 minute. Remove from the wok or skillet and transfer to a deep serving dish.
5 Heat the remaining oil in the wok or skillet over medium-high heat. Add the garlic and stir-fry until fragrant, about 30 seconds. Add the reserved seafood, broccoli, and yellow bean paste; stir-fry until the shrimp turns pink, about 3 minutes. Add the chicken stock, oyster sauce, fish sauce, and sugar and bring to a boil. Add the all-purpose cornstarch mixture slowly until the sauce slightly thickens, about 1 minute.
6 Dish out the seafood stir-fry mixture on top of noodles. Garnish with green onions and fresh coriander leaves.

Spicy Peanut Noodles with Fresh Coriander Leaves

I wanted to create a Thai version of Chinese sesame peanut noodles and came up with this fabulous recipe. It's perfect for picnics and potlucks because you can make it in advance and it can be served at room temperature. For a vegan version of this recipe, substitute the chicken stock with vegetable broth and the fish sauce with soy sauce.

SERVES 4–6 AS PART OF A MULTI-COURSE MEAL
PREPARATION TIME: 10 MINUTES
COOKING TIME: 11 MINUTES

8 oz (250 g) dried linguini
1 teaspoon sesame oil
½ cup (28 g) fresh coriander leaves (cilantro) plus more for garnish

SAUCE
1 tablespoon high-heat cooking oil
1 garlic clove, minced
1 small shallot, finely sliced
1 teaspoon minced galangal or fresh ginger
1 fresh red or green chili, preferably Thai, deseeded and finely sliced
1 teaspoon thick red curry paste
½ teaspoon ground turmeric
½ cup (120 g) creamy peanut butter
¾ cup (185 ml) coconut milk
½ cup (125 ml) Basic Chicken Stock (page 26) or store-bought
½ tablespoon fish sauce (nam pla)
1 teaspoon freshly squeezed lime juice
1 teaspoon palm or brown sugar

1 Sauce: Heat the oil in a medium saucepan over medium-high heat. Add the garlic, shallots, glangal, and chili, and stir-fry until fragrant, about 1 minute Reduce heat to medium. Add the red curry paste, and turmeric, stirring to break up the paste, about 1 minute. Add peanut butter, coconut milk, chicken stock, fish sauce, lime juice, and palm sugar; bring to a gentle boil, stirring frequently. Remove from the heat and whisk until smooth.
2 Prepare the linguini according to package directions. Drain the linguini and rinse with cool water. Toss the noodles with the sesame oil. Add Sauce and toss to combine. If you prefer a thinner sauce use more of the chicken stock. Add fresh coriander leaves and toss. Transfer the noodles to a serving platter and garnish with fresh coriander leaves. Serve warm or at room temperature.

COOK'S NOTE: Substitute with 12 oz (350 g) fresh flat rice noodles if you prefer. Bring a large pot of water to a boil. Remove from heat. Immerse noodles in hot water; let stand 10 minutes, stirring occasionally. Soak until noodles are soft, yet firm. Drain well and rinse with cool water.

Pad Thai

Everyone's favorite Thai noodle dish, Pad Thai, was made a national Thai dish in the 1930's when prime minister Luang Phibunsongkhram launched a campaign to reduce rice consumption. Tired of constantly eating out, my friends begged me to create a simple Pad Thai recipe and here it is…no reservations required!

SERVES 3 AS A MAIN DISH OR 4–6 AS PART OF A MULTI-COURSE MEAL
PREPARATION TIME: 10 MINUTES + SOAKING TIME
COOKING TIME: 10 MINUTES

8 oz (250 g) dried rice stick noodles
⅓ cup (80 ml) tamarind concentrate
¼ cup (65 ml) + 2 tablespoons fish sauce (nam pla)
2 tablespoons rice or white vinegar
½ cup (85 g) palm or brown sugar
1 teaspoon paprika
2 tablespoons high-heat cooking oil
2 garlic cloves, minced
12 medium shrimp, shelled and deveined
4 oz (100 g) firm tofu, drained and cubed
1 egg, lightly beaten
½ cup (50 g) bean sprouts, ends trimmed
Shredded carrots for garnish
Shredded red cabbage for garnish
Fresh coriander leaves (cilantro) for garnish
Lime wedges
4 tablespoons crushed roasted peanuts

1 Bring a large pot of water to a boil. Remove from the heat. Immerse the noodles in hot water and let stand 10 minutes, stirring occasionally. Soak until the noodles are soft, yet firm. Drain well and rinse with cool water.
2 In a small bowl, combine the tamarind concentrate, fish sauce, vinegar, palm sugar, and paprika. Set aside.
3 Heat the oil in a wok or skillet over medium-high heat. Add garlic and stir-fry until garlic is fragrant, about 30 seconds. Add shrimp, tofu, and egg. Stir-fry for 2 minutes, until egg is scrambled and shrimp turns pink. Add reserved rice noodles and tamarind mixture. Stir-fry for 2–3 minutes, tossing to combine all of the ingredients. Transfer to a platter and garnish with small piles of bean sprouts, carrot, and red cabbage on the sides of the platter. Sprinkle peanuts and fresh coriander leaves over the top. Serve immediately with lime wedges.

Glass Noodles with Egg, Beef and Bean Sprouts
(Beef Pad Woon Sen)

My kids love this dish because it's relatively mild (I omit the chili when I make this for my toddler twins). This light and savory cousin to Pad Thai, is a similar stir-fry noodle dish but uses clear, glass or cellophane noodles instead of the thicker rice stick noodles. You can you use any combination of meat and vegetables in this dish. Because glass or vermicelli noodles are made from mung beans, this is a fantastic low-carb or gluten-free option.

SERVES 3 AS A MAIN DISH OR 4–6 AS PART OF A MULTI-COURSE MEAL
PREPARATION TIME: 20 MINUTES + SOAKING TIME
COOKING TIME: 10 MINUTES

8 oz (250 g) beef tenderloin, flank steak or top sirloin, thinly sliced
½ teaspoon all-purpose cornstarch
1 teaspoon + 1 tablespoon soy sauce, divided
¼ teaspoon white pepper
1 teaspoon + 2 tablespoons high-heat cooking oil, divided
4 oz (100 g) dried glass noodles
2 eggs
½ teaspoon salt
Pinch of white pepper
2 garlic cloves, minced
½ small onion, thinly sliced
1 fresh hot red or green chili, preferably Thai (deseeded for less heat), finely sliced
½ cup (46 g) red pepper, thinly sliced
½ cup (50 g) bean sprouts, ends trimmed
4 teaspoons fish sauce (nam pla)
1 tablespoon oyster sauce
2 teaspoons palm or brown sugar
½ cup (125 ml) water
Fresh coriander leaves (cilantro) for garnish

1 Toss beef with all-purpose cornstarch, 1 teaspoon soy sauce, pepper, and 1 teaspoon oil. Cover and let sit at room temperature for 10 minutes.

2 Bring a large pot of water to a boil. Remove from the heat. Immerse the noodles in hot water; let stand for 3–5 minutes stirring occasionally. Soak until the noodles are soft, yet firm. Drain well.

3 In a medium bowl, whisk together eggs, salt, and pepper. Add the remaining 1 tablespoon of oil in the wok or skillet over medium-high heat. Cook the eggs, stirring, until set but still moist. Transfer the eggs to a plate. Wash and thoroughly dry the wok or skillet.

4 Heat the remaining 1 tablespoon oil in the wok or skillet over medium-high heat. Add the garlic, onion, and chili; stir-fry until the garlic is fragrant and the onion is translucent, about 1 minute. Add reserved beef and red pepper and stir-fry for 2 minutes. Add reserved eggs, bean sprouts, fish sauce, soy sauce, oyster sauce, palm sugar, and water; stir-fry for 2 minutes. Add the noodles and stir-fry for 1 minute. Transfer to a serving platter and garnish with fresh coriander leaves. Serve immediately.

Crab Fried Rice

This simple, yet elegant fried rice brings me back to the sunny beaches of Phuket where crab is fresh and plentiful. The heat from the chili is balanced by bursts of sweet peas intermingled with succulent pieces of crab. Thai people like to season their rice with a table sauce called nam pla prik, which is a combination of fish sauce, a squeeze of lime juice, and a few slices of chili peppers. For best results, rice should be chilled in a refrigerator over night before cooking this dish.

SERVES 4–6 AS PART OF A MULTI-COURSE MEAL
PREPARATION TIME: 10 MINUTES
COOKING TIME: 10 MINUTES

2 eggs
¼ teaspoon salt
Pinch of white pepper
2 tablespoons high-heat cooking oil, divided
1 garlic clove, minced
1 small shallot, finely sliced
1 fresh hot red or green chili, preferably Thai (deseeded if you prefer less heat), finely sliced
3 cups (450 g) cooked and chilled Thai jasmine rice

4 teaspoons oyster sauce
1 tablespoon soy sauce
1 teaspoon palm or brown sugar
8 oz (250 g) crab meat, picked over for shells
½ cup (73 g) fresh or thawed frozen peas
½ cup (50 g) finely chopped green onions (green and white parts) plus more for garnish
4 tablespoons finely chopped fresh coriander leaves (cilantro)
4 tablespoons finely chopped Thai or Italian basil
Lime wedges

1 In a medium bowl, whisk together the eggs, salt, and pepper.

2 In a wok or skillet, heat ½ of the oil over medium heat. Cook eggs, stirring, until set but still moist. Transfer eggs to a plate. Wash and thoroughly dry the wok or skillet.

3 Heat the remaining oil over medium-high heat. Add the garlic, shallots, and chili and stir-fry until fragrant, about 1 minute. Add rice and stir-fry for 2 minutes. Add oyster sauce, soy sauce, and palm sugar; stir-fry for 2 minutes. Add the crab meat and peas; stir-fry for 1 minute. Return eggs to the wok and add green onions, fresh coriander, and basil leaves; stir-fry for 30 seconds.

4 Dish out onto serving bowl and garnish with green onions. Serve immediately with lime wedges.

Spicy Fried Rice

This is a staple dish in Thai cuisine and is simple and fast. Feel free to add any cooked meat or some cubed tofu to this dish for added protein. Adjust the amount of chili sauce to your liking. I like to balance this dish with a sweet dish such as Crispy Mango Coconut Chicken (page 69) along with a Mango Shake (page 135). For best results, the rice should be chilled overnight in the refrigerator before cooking this dish.

SERVES 4–6 AS PART OF A MULTI-COURSE MEAL
PREPARATION TIME: 10 MINUTES
COOKING TIME: 10 MINUTES

2 large eggs
1 teaspoon salt, divided
Pinch of freshly ground white pepper
2 tablespoons oil, divided
1 garlic clove, minced
1 small shallot, finely sliced
3 cups (450 g) cooked and chilled Thai jasmine rice
4 teaspoons fish sauce (nam pla)
1 tablespoon soy sauce
1 tablespoon palm or brown sugar
8 oz (250 g) firm tofu, drained, patted dry and cubed
½ cup (46 g) red bell pepper, diced
2–4 teaspoons Asian chili sauce (preferably Sriracha)
4 tablespoons finely chopped fresh coriander leaves
   (cilantro) plus more for garnish
Finely chopped green onions (green and white parts) for
   garnish

1. Whisk together the eggs, ½ teaspoon of the salt and the pinch of the pepper In a medium bowl.
2 Heat ½ of the oil in a wok or skillet over medium heat. Cook the eggs, stirring until set but still moist. Transfer the eggs to a plate. Wash and thoroughly dry the wok or skillet.
3 Heat the remaining oil over medium-high heat. Add garlic and shallots and stir-fry until fragrant, about 1 minute. Add rice and stir-fry for 2 minutes. Add fish sauce, soy sauce, palm sugar, and the remaining ½ teaspoon salt and stir-fry for 2 minutes. Add the tofu and red pepper; stir-fry for 1 minute. Add the reserved eggs, chili sauce, and fresh coriander leaves and stir-fry for 30 seconds.
4 Dish onto a serving bowl and garnish with fresh coriander leaves and green onions.

Sweet and Tangy Thai Noodles
(Mee Krob)

Mee Krob literally translates as "crisp noodles" and is considered a Palace dish in Thailand. Mee Krob is like a light crispy noodle cloud topped with crunchy bean sprouts, tender pork, and eggs, in a sweet, sour, and tangy sauce. The rice vermicelli noodles puff up very quickly as does the egg ribbon and my friends like to gather around the kitchen to watch them both come to life as they hit the hot oil.

SERVES 3 AS A MAIN DISH OR 4–6 AS PART OF A MULTI-COURSE MEAL
PREPARATION TIME: 15 MINUTES
COOKING TIME: 25 MINUTES

3 cups (50 ml) oil for frying
6 oz (175 g) rice vermicelli noodles, crushed in a plastic bag
2 large eggs, beaten
4 oz (100 g) firm tofu, drained, patted dry and cubed
4 garlic cloves, minced
2 small shallots, thinly sliced
4 tablespoons finely chopped green onions (white and green parts)
1 fresh hot red or green chili, preferably Thai (deseeded if you prefer less heat), finely sliced
4 oz (100 g) pork tenderloin, cut into bite-sized pieces
4 oz (100 g) medium shrimp, shelled and deveined

SAUCE
2 medium tomatoes, finely chopped
½ cup (125 ml) tamarind water (4 teaspoons tamarind concentrate mixed with ½ cup hot water)
4 tablespoons freshly squeezed lime juice
4 tablespoons palm or brown sugar
8 kaffir lime leaves, sliced into threads/shreds (optional)
2 tablespoons fish sauce (nam pla)
4 tablespoons finely chopped fresh coriander leaves (cilantro) for garnish
4 tablespoons bean sprouts for garnish

1 Heat 2–3 inches (5–7.5 cm) of the oil to 375°F (190°C) in a wok or deep skillet. Fry the noodles in small batches until they puff up and turn light to golden brown. Flip the noodles frequently to rotate them while heating. Remove the noodles with a metal strainer to a paper towel-lined sheet pan. Transfer to a serving platter and set aside.
2 Drizzle the eggs into the oil to form a ribbon of cooked egg. Remove and drain on a paper towel-lined sheet pan. Chop the egg into small pieces.
3 Fry the tofu until golden brown, about 4 minutes. Drain on a paper towel-lined sheet pan and set aside.
4 Sauce: Place the tomato, tamarind water, lime juice, palm sugar, kaffir lime leaves (if using), and fish sauce in small bowl. Toss to combine. Transfer to a medium saucepan over medium-high heat and bring to a boil. Reduce heat to medium-low and let it simmer until it thickens, about 3 minutes. Keep warm.
5 Discard all but 1 tablespoon of oil from the wok or skillet. Heat oil on medium-high heat. Add the garlic, shallots, onions, and chili. Stir-fry until the garlic is fragrant and the onions are translucent, about 1 minute. Add the pork and shrimp and stir-fry until the pork turns white and the shrimp turns pink. Add the reserved egg ribbons and stir-fry for 1 minute. Remove from the heat.
6 Place the noodles on a platter. Dish out contents of the wok or skillet and place on top of noodles. Ladle the Sauce over the top. Place the tofu on top of the Sauce. Garnish with fresh coriander leaves and bean sprouts. Serve immediately.

COOK'S NOTE: Don't confuse rice vermicelli noodles, which are made of rice flour, with Chinese vermicelli noodles also known as dried glass noodles.

Sweet and Tangy Thai Noodles

Pineapple Fried Rice

Pineapple fried rice is my absolute favorite and my husband and I loved eating it throughout Thailand where pineapples are abundant thanks to its lush tropical climate. It's no surprise then that Pineapple Fried Rice is one of this most popular of all Thai dishes. This vibrant, colorful dish is fun to include on a dinner party menu because you serve it in a hollowed out pineapple shell! It's also a great recipe for leftovers as you can use any cooked meat. For best results, the rice should be chilled in a refrigerator overnight before cooking this dish.

SERVES 4–6 AS PART OF A MULTI-COURSE MEAL
PREPARATION TIME: 15 MINUTES
COOKING TIME: 10 MINUTES

1 whole pineapple
2 large eggs
1 teaspoon salt, divided
Pinch of ground white pepper
2 tablespoons high-heat cooking oil, divided
1 garlic clove, minced
1 small shallot, finely sliced
1 fresh hot red or green chili, preferably Thai (deseeded if you prefer less heat), finely sliced
3 cups (450 g) cooked and chilled Thai jasmine rice
2 tablespoons fish sauce (nam pla)
1 tablespoon soy sauce
1 cup (150 g) cubed cooked chicken breast
1 cup (150 g) cubed cooked shrimp
½ cup (73 g) fresh or thawed frozen peas
4 tablespoons finely chopped fresh coriander leaves (cilantro) plus more for garnish
4 tablespoons finely chopped fresh mint

1 Cut the pineapple in half lengthwise and cut the fruit from the middle, leaving shell halves intact. Cut out the eyes and core. Set the shell halves aside. Dice the fruit. Dry the diced pineapple with paper towels and set aside.
2 In a medium bowl, whisk together the eggs, ½ teaspoon of the salt, and the pinch of pepper.
3 Heat ½ of the oil in a wok or large skillet over medium-high heat. Cook eggs, stirring, until set but still moist. Transfer eggs to a plate. Wash and thoroughly dry the wok or skillet.
4 Heat the remaining oil over medium-high heat. Add the garlic, shallots and chili and stir-fry until fragrant, about 30 seconds. Add the rice and stir-fry for 2 minutes. Add the fish sauce, soy sauce, chicken, shrimp, peas, and the remaining ½ teaspoon salt and stir fry for 2–3 minutes. Add the reserved eggs, pineapple, fresh coriander leaves, and mint; stir-fry for 30 seconds.
5 Scoop the fried rice into the pineapple shells and garnish with fresh coriander leaves. Serve immediately.

COOK'S NOTE: If you dice the pineapple ahead of time, rinse the pineapple shells with boiling water and dry with paper towels before serving.

CHAPTER EIGHT

Vegetables and Tofu

My husband has the green thumb in our family so he tends to our small, yet abundant crop of green beans, zucchini, tomatoes, bok choy, lemongrass, and Asian herb garden. I'm really good at the picking and cooking; the planting, um, not so much.

Whether you pluck veggies from your own garden or rely on your grocery store or farmer's market, the simplest Thai vegetable dishes are the best. If you use vegetables at the peak of freshness and stir-fry them to tender-crisp perfection in a hot wok or skillet you really can't go wrong. Create a lustrous glaze from a simple combination of Thai seasonings, sherry, a bit of chili, and some brown sugar or sauté them in a tangy and sour tamarind sauce and your vegetables will come alive in a way you've never experienced. I made the Asparagus, Shiitake, Mushrooms, and Tofu (page 120) dish the other day and I couldn't stop eating it. Literally. I ate the whole dish and had to make another one before my family came home for dinner.

The Thailand landscape is dotted with gardens filled with vegetables and aromatic herbs. The Thai diet is based primarily on rice, noodles, and vegetables with poultry, meats, and seafood playing a secondary role. Silky tofu is eaten all over Thailand as an inexpensive means of protein. Tofu absorbs all of the bold, piquant, and varied flavors in Thai cooking making it a great choice for stir-fries and other dishes. Trying Meatless Mondays on for size? Well, this will be your go-to chapter.

One of my other favorites is the Thai Garlicky Eggplant (page 122), it oozes with garlicky goodness and sweet notes from the Oyster sauce. The Green Beans and Tofu with Garlic Sauce (page 121) has a unique crunchy texture because the tofu is flash fried in a dusting of all-purpose cornstarch. I'm also so honored to include Chef Hong's Winter Squash Curry recipe (page 123) from her fabulous New York Thai eatery, Ngam.

Chinese Broccoli and Cashew Nuts

Chinese broccoli, or *gai lan*, is a leafy green vegetable which has a peppery bite with a hint of sweetness. It can be found at Asian markets and some specialty markets. At Chinese dim sum restaurants, they cut the broccoli at the table in front of you with a pair of scissors followed by a quick drizzle of oyster sauce. This preparation melds together classic Thai flavors with the sweet crunch of cashews sprinkled on top.

SERVES 4 AS PART OF A MULTI-COURSE MEAL
PREPARATION TIME: 5 MINUTES
COOKING TIME: 8 MINUTES

2 tablespoons cooking oil
2 garlic cloves, minced
1 fresh hot red or green chili, preferably Thai (deseeded if you prefer less heat), finely sliced
12 oz (350 g) Chinese broccoli, end of stems trimmed
1 teaspoon cooking sherry
¼ cup (65 ml) Basic Chicken Stock (page 26) or store-bought
4 teaspoons oyster sauce
2 teaspoons palm or brown sugar
¼ cup (34 g) cashew nuts

1 Heat the oil in the wok or skillet over medium-high heat. Add the garlic and chili and stir-fry until fragrant, about 30 seconds. Add the Chinese broccoli and sherry and stir-fry for 1 minute.
2 Add the chicken stock, close the lid and let cook for 4–5 minutes or until the broccoli is tender.
3 Add the oyster sauce and palm sugar; stir-fry, tossing to coat, for 1 minute. Dish onto a serving platter and cut the broccoli into 3 sections with kitchen shears. Top with cashews and serve immediately with jasmine rice.

COOK'S NOTE: You may substitute with broccoli rabe if you can't find Chinese broccoli.

Spinach, Mushrooms, and Bean Sprouts

If Popeye were Thai, this would be his favorite recipe. A terrific side dish, this recipe is so simple and is loaded with nutrients from the spinach and mushrooms. Feel free to experiment with a combination of mushrooms and add some Sriracha for a kick.

SERVES 4 AS PART OF A MULTI-COURSE MEAL
PREPARATION TIME: 10 MINUTES
COOKING TIME: 8 MINUTES

2 tablespoons high-heat cooking oil
1 garlic clove, minced
1 teaspoon minced galangal or ginger
1 fresh hot red or green chili, preferably Thai (deseeded if you prefer less heat), finely sliced
4 oz (100 g) fresh shiitake mushrooms, stemmed and thinly sliced
4 oz (100 g) canned straw mushrooms, drained and halved
1 teaspoon cooking sherry
6 oz (175 g) spinach leaves, trimmed and cleaned
1 tablespoon fish sauce (nam pla)
1 tablespoon oyster sauce
1 tablespoon palm or brown sugar
1 cup (100 g) bean sprouts, ends trimmed

1 Heat the oil in the wok or skillet over medium-high heat.
2 Add the garlic, galangal, and chili; stir-fry until fragrant, about 30 seconds. Add the mushrooms and sherry and stir-fry for 2 minutes. Add the spinach and stir-fry for 2 minutes or until spinach is wilted. Add the fish sauce, oyster sauce, palm sugar, and bean sprouts; stir-fry for 30 seconds. Dish out and serve immediately with jasmine rice.

Stir-fried Vegetables with Chili-Tamarind Sauce

The bright, sweet and sour flavors of tamarind come alive in this simple stir-fried veggie dish. Use whatever fresh vegetables you like but I think this colorful combo has great mix of flavor and texture. You can also add your favorite meat to turn this side kick into a main event. My friend Terry likes to add diced tofu and edamame for a boost of soy protein especially when she knows she'll be working out later that day.

SERVES 4–6 AS PART OF A MULTI-COURSE MEAL
PREPARATION TIME: 10 MINUTES + BLANCHING TIME
COOKING TIME: 10 MINUTES

2 tablespoons high-heat cooking oil
1 garlic clove, minced
1 tablespoon minced galangal or ginger
2 oz (50 g) sliced carrots
2 oz (50 g) stemmed and sliced fresh shiitake mushrooms
2 oz (50 g) thinly sliced red bell pepper
2 oz (50 g) snow peas, tips and strings removed, cut into 1 in (2.5 cm) pieces on a diagonal
2 oz (50 g) broccoli florets
2 oz (50 g) canned baby corn, drained, rinsed, and sliced lengthwise
¾ cup (15 g) fresh Thai or Italian basil leaves

SAUCE
1½ teaspoons tamarind concentrate
2 tablespoons vegetable stock or water
1½ tablespoons palm or brown sugar
1½ tablespoons fish sauce (nam pla)
1½ teaspoons Asian chili sauce, preferably Sriracha

1 Sauce: Whisk together the tamarind concentrate, vegetable broth or water, palm sugar, fish sauce, and chili sauce in small bowl. Set aside.
2 Cook snow peas and broccoli florets in boiling water until tender, about 1 minute.

Using a slotted spoon, transfer the snow peas and broccoli to an ice bath until cool. Drain and set aside
3 Heat the oil in the wok or skillet over high heat. Add the garlic and galangal to the wok or skillet and stir-fry until fragrant, about 30 seconds. Add the carrot and mushrooms and stir-fry for 3 minutes. Add the red bell pepper and stir-fry for 1 minute. Add the reserved snow peas, broccoli, and baby corn; stir-fry for 1 minute. Add the Sauce and stir-fry for 1 minute. Add the basil leaves and stir-fry for 30 seconds or until the basil is wilted. Dish out and serve with jasmine rice.

COOK'S NOTE: If you can't find tamarind concentrate, use lemon or lime juice with a touch of brown sugar.

Asparagus, Shiitake Mushrooms, and Tofu

This is my friend JJ's favorite dish. An avid runner who loves fresh veggies and soy protein. I love the simplicity of this recipe. The salty and sweet flavors from the fish sauce and oyster sauce come together beautifully with the heat from the chili. A touch of sherry enhances the flavors and aroma in this dish resulting in a gorgeous vegetarian feast or side dish.

SERVES 6 AS PART OF A MULTI-COURSE MEAL
PREPARATION TIME: 10 MINUTES
COOKING TIME: 10 MINUTES

2 tablespoons high-heat cooking oil
8 oz (250 g) firm tofu, drained, patted dry and cubed
1 garlic clove, minced
1 small shallot, finely sliced
1 fresh hot red or green chili, preferably Thai (deseeded if you prefer less heat), finely sliced
8 oz (250 g) fresh asparagus, ends trimmed and sliced diagonally into 1 in (2.5 cm) pieces
2 teaspoons cooking sherry
6 fresh shiitake mushrooms, stemmed and thinly sliced
2 tablespoons fish sauce
1 tablespoon oyster sauce
1 tablespoon palm or brown sugar

1 Heat ½ of the oil in the wok or skillet over medium-high heat. Add the tofu pieces and stir-fry until golden brown, about 3 minutes. Remove from the pan and set aside.
2 Heat the remaining oil in the wok or skillet over medium-high heat. Add the garlic, shallots, and chili and stir-fry until fragrant, about 30 seconds. Add the asparagus and stir-fry for 2 minutes. Add the sherry and mushrooms and stir-fry for 1 minute. Add the reserved tofu, fish sauce, oyster sauce, and palm sugar; stir-fry for 30 seconds. Dish out and serve immediately with jasmine rice.

Green Beans and Tofu with Garlic Sauce

This is a spicy dish with a unique texture. The tofu is flash fried in a mixture of flour and cornstarch giving it a nice crispy crunch with every bite. This is another great meatless option filled with complex flavors and is chock full of soy protein.

SERVES 4 AS PART OF A MULTI-COURSE MEAL
PREPARATION TIME: 10 MINUTES + BLANCHING TIME
COOKING TIME: 15 MINUTES

8 oz (250 g) yard-long beans or green beans,
　　cut into 1 in (2.5 cm) pieces
2 tablespoons flour
2 tablespoons all-purpose cornstarch
½ teaspoon salt
Oil for frying
8 oz (250 g) firm tofu, drained, patted dry, and
　　cut into cubes
1 garlic clove, minced
½ small white onion, cut into small chunks
½ teaspoon Asian chili-garlic sauce, preferably
　　sambal oelek
2 teaspoons soy sauce
2 teaspoons oyster sauce
1 teaspoon palm or brown sugar
¾ cup (15 g) fresh Thai or Italian basil leaves

1 Cook the green beans in boiling water until tender-crisp, about 5 minutes. Transfer the beans with a slotted spoon to an ice bath until cool. Drain. Set aside.
2 Combine the flour, all-purpose cornstarch, and salt in a bowl. Toss tofu pieces into the flour-cornstarch mixture. In a wok or deep skillet, heat the oil to 375°F (190°C). Fry the tofu for 4 minutes. Flip the tofu and fry for another 4 minutes to a golden brown on all sides. Drain on a paper towel-lined sheet pan. Set aside.
3 Remove all but 1 tablespoon oil from the wok or skillet. Heat oil to medium-high heat. Add the garlic, and onion; stir-fry until the garlic is fragrant and the onion is translucent, about 1 minute. Add the reserved tofu and stir-fry for 1 minute. Add the reserved green beans, chili-garlic sauce, soy sauce, oyster sauce, and palm sugar; stir-fry for 1 minute. Add the basil and stir-fry for 30 seconds or until basil is wilted. Dish out and serve immediately with jasmine rice.

Thai Garlicky Eggplant

Asian eggplant are narrow in shape, have thinner skin and tend to be sweeter than American eggplant. The eggplant absorbs all of the garlicky goodness in this dish so each bite is like a flavor bomb. Rich, complex, sweet, and spicy, this side dish is definitely "da bomb" in my book.

SERVES 4 AS PART OF A MULTI-COURSE MEAL
PREPARATION TIME: 10 MINUTES
COOKING TIME: 10 MINUTES

3 tablespoons high-heat cooking oil, divided
8 oz (250 g) Asian eggplants, Cut ½ lengthwise and then slice crosswise into wedges
1 tablespoon soy sauce
3 garlic cloves, minced
½ small white onion, finely sliced
1 fresh hot red or green chili, preferably Thai (deseeded if you prefer less heat), finely sliced
¼ cup (65 ml) vegetable stock or water
1 tablespoon oyster sauce
2 tablespoons fish sauce (nam pla)
1 tablespoon palm or brown sugar
2 teaspoons all-purpose cornstarch mixed with 2 tablespoons water
¾ cup (15 g) fresh Thai or Italian basil leaves

1 Heat 2 tablespoons of the oil in the wok or skillet over moderately high heat. Add the eggplant and soy sauce and stir-fry for 3 minutes. Remove from pan set aside. Add the remaining 1 tablespoon oil.
2 Add the garlic, onion, and chili and stir-fry until fragrant and the onion is translucent, about 1 minute. Add the reserved eggplant and vegetable stock or water and stir-fry for 2 minutes or until the eggplant is tender.
3 Add the oyster sauce, fish sauce, and palm sugar; stir-fry for 1 minute. Add the cornstarch mixture and stir-fry until thickened, about 30 seconds. Add the basil leaves and stir-fry for 30 seconds until the basil is wilted.
4 Dish out and serve immediately with jasmine rice.

Winter Squash Curry

I was lucky enough to enjoy this amazing dish at Chef Hong Thaimee's restaurant, Ngam, in the East Village, New York. Chef Hong had stints at Jean Georges Spice Market and Perry St. before opening her own restaurant and she graciously shares this signature dish with us.

SERVES 4–6 AS PART OF A MULTI-COURSE MEAL
PREPARATION TIME: 10 MINUTES + BLANCHING TIME
COOKING TIME: 10 MINUTES

4 cups (700 g) winter squash (butternut squash, kabocha pumpkin, etc), diced
4 tablespoons thick red curry paste
3 cups (750 ml) coconut milk
One 16 oz (500 g) block firm tofu, drained, patted dry and cut into ½ in (1.25 cm) cubes
4 tablespoons sliced long red chili
¼ cup (5 g) fresh Thai or Italian basil leaves
1½ teaspoons salt
1½ teaspoons palm or brown sugar

1 Cook the squash in boiling water until tender, about 4–5 minutes. Using a slotted spoon, transfer the squash to an ice bath until cool. Drain and set aside.
2 In a saucepan, mix the curry paste and about ¼ cup (65 ml) of the coconut milk. Cook for about 2–3 minutes over medium-high heat until fragrant.
3 Add the squash and the remaining coconut milk. Let it simmer for about 5 minutes or until boiling.
4 Add the tofu, chili, and Thai basil leaves. Stir ingredients carefully so as not to break the tofu. Stir in the salt and palm sugar. Dish out and serve immediately with jasmine rice.

Winter Squash Curry

Spicy Thai Tofu with Spinach, Basil, and Peanuts

When I was pregnant with our twins I was looking for interesting ways to eat get more folic acid and was tired of eating spinach salads. I was also craving flavor and needed extra protein to keep my energy up. After all, I was eating for three! I came up with this tasty and spicy recipe loaded with spinach, tofu, and crunchy peanuts. Every time I ate this I remember lots of kicking in my tummy, so I would say it garnered six thumbs up all around.

SERVES 6 AS PART OF A MULTI-COURSE MEAL
PREPARATION TIME: 10 MINUTES
COOKING TIME: 8 MINUTES

2 tablespoons high-heat cooking oil, divided
One 16 oz (500 g) block firm tofu, drained, patted dry and cut into ½ in (1.25 cm) cubes
2 garlic cloves, minced
1 tablespoon minced galangal or fresh ginger
8 oz (250 g) spinach, washed and trimmed

1½ tablespoons fish sauce (nam pla)
2 teaspoons cooking sherry
1 tablespoon oyster sauce
1 tablespoon palm or brown sugar
2 teaspoons freshly squeezed lime juice
2 teaspoons Asian chili sauce, preferably Sriracha
½ cup (10 g) finely chopped fresh Thai or Italian basil
⅓ cup (50 g) crushed roasted peanuts plus more for garnish
Fresh Thai or Italian basil leaves for garnish

1 Heat ½ of the oil in a wok or skillet over medium-high heat. Add the tofu pieces and stir-fry until golden brown, about 3 minutes. Remove from the pan and set aside.
2 Heat the remaining oil in the wok or skillet over medium-high heat. Add the garlic and galangal and stir-fry until fragrant, about 30 seconds. Add the spinach, fish sauce, sherry, oyster sauce, palm sugar, lime juice, and chili sauce; stir-fry until the spinach is wilted, about 2 minutes. Add the basil leaves and peanuts and stir-fry for 30 seconds until basil is wilted. Dish out and garnish with basil leaves and peanuts. Serve with jasmine rice.

Thai Tofu with Summer Squash Red Bell Pepper and Lime

Our garden explodes with zucchini over the summer and I sigh whenever my husband unloads another armful onto our kitchen counter. I don't mean to sound ungrateful but I was running out of ideas until I came up with this hearty yet light tofu curry dish filled with zucchini and colorful bell pepper with a tangy lime finish.

SERVES 4 AS PART OF A MULTI-COURSE MEAL
PREPARATION TIME: 10 MINUTES
COOKING TIME: 15 MINUTES

2 tablespoons high-heat cooking oil, divided
8 oz (250 g) firm tofu, drained, patted dry and cut into bite-sized cubes
1 garlic clove, minced
1 tablespoon minced galangal or fresh ginger
1 teaspoon thick red curry paste
4 yellow or green zucchini, diced (3 cups/100 g)
2 red bell pepper, diced (2 cups/100 g)
1 cup (250 ml) coconut milk
½ cup (125 ml) Basic Chicken Stock (page 26) or store-bought
1 tablespoon freshly squeezed lime juice
2 tablespoons fish sauce (nam pla)
1 teaspoon palm or brown sugar
½ teaspoon crushed red pepper flakes
¾ cup (15 g) fresh Thai or Italian basil leaves

1 Heat ½ of the oil in a wok or skillet over medium-high heat. Add the tofu pieces and stir-fry until golden brown, about 3 minutes. Remove from pan and set aside.

2 Heat the remaining oil in the wok or skillet over medium-high heat. Add the garlic and galangal and stir-fry until fragrant, about 30 seconds. Reduce heat to medium. Add the curry paste and stir-fry, stirring to break it up, about 1 minute. Add the zucchini and red bell pepper and stir-fry for 3 minutes. Add the reserved tofu, coconut milk, chicken stock, lime juice, fish sauce, palm sugar, and red pepper flakes. Bring to a gentle boil. Reduce to medium-low and simmer for 5–7 minutes. Add basil leaves and cook for 30 seconds or until basil is wilted. Dish out and serve with jasmine rice.

CHAPTER NINE

Desserts

I'll never forget my first bite of Sticky Rice with Mango during a monsoon-like downfall in Chiang Mai. We ducked into a tiny café and ordered this creamy, coconutty and sticky dessert with fresh ripe mango. I couldn't believe something so simple could be so divine and memorable. I was inspired to recreate Sweet, Ripe Mango with Sticky Rice (page 131) for my friends and am so happy to share it now with you.

Thai people embrace all food, including sweets, but they don't typically follow their dinner meal with a dessert. They enjoy sweets throughout the day and as they do their snacks.

Whether you plan to serve these sweet treats at the end of a meal or prefer to serve as a snack like they do in Thailand, your family's sweet tooth is in for a treat. Banana Spring Rolls (page 138) are so quick to prepare and the infusion of lemongrass in the chocolate sauce lends a bright, citrusy note. The Banana, Kiwi and Passion Fruit Salad (page 130) is surprisingly spicy yet soothing with hints of mint. My children wouldn't forgive me if I didn't include ice cream. Bravo TV's Top Chef Desserts' finalist and owner of Bittersweet Treats, Danielle Keene, has graciously given us her creamy and delicious Thai-inspired Coconut Thai Basil Ice Cream recipe (page 134). This Dessert Diva's luscious and exotic ice cream recipe is a cinch to make in your ice cream maker.

Quenching your thirst and tempering the hot and spicy flavors during a Thai meal is easy with a cooling, smooth and creamy Mango Shake (page 135) or with sweet and rich Thai Iced Tea (page 136). I also love creating Thai-inspired drinks based on popular American favorites like Lemongrass Ginger Ale (page 136) or Thai Basil Lemon Soda (page 135). Sipping soda will take on a whole new meaning.

How to Make Coconut Cream Custard in Banana Leaf Bowls

1 Measure the custard ingredients and place into individual bowls.

4 Form banana leaf strips into a cross.

2 Cut the banana leaves into 2 x 6 inches (5 x 16 cm) long strips.

5 Pour the mixture into the ramekins, filling each one ¾ full.

3 Press two banana leaf strips into each ramekin.

6 Bake the custards for 40–45 minutes or until custard is set.

Coconut Cream Custard in Banana Leaf Bowls

I have a lot of friends who are lactose intolerant (including myself), so I love to make desserts with coconut milk because it's naturally dairy-free. Creamy and luscious, this simple and elegant custard is heavenly and beautifully presented in a banana leaf shell and topped with a glistening mango glaze. If you can't find banana leaves, it's still a beautiful dessert served simply in a ramekin.

MAKES 4 SERVINGS
PREPARATION TIME: 10 MINUTES
COOKING TIME: 45 MINUTES

Oil, to grease ramekins
Banana leaves
1 cup (250 ml) coconut milk
¼ cup (50 g) sugar
2 large eggs
1 ripe banana, cut into chunks
1 teaspoon coconut or vanilla extract

MANGO SAUCE
1 cup (250 ml) puréed mango
½ cup (100 g) sugar
1 tablespoon all-purpose cornstarch
¾ cup (185 ml) water

1 Preheat oven to 325°F (160°C). Grease the ramekins with a bit of oil. Cut two banana leaf strips about 2 x 6 inches (5 x 15 cm) long for each ramekin and press into the ramekin in the form of a cross (as a lining)
2 Place coconut milk, sugar, eggs, bananas, and coconut extract in a blender or food processor. Blend or process for 30 seconds. Pour the mixture into the ramekins, filling each one ¾ full.
3 Place ramekins in a flat-bottomed glass dish. Fill this dish part-way with boiling water (⅓ to ½ way up the side of the ramekins). Gently place the dish in the oven, being careful not to spill the water. Bake for 40–45 minutes or until the custard has set.
4 Meanwhile, make the Mango Sauce: Combine all of the ingredients for the sauce in a small saucepan. Whisk until lump free. Place over medium heat, stirring constantly. Bring to a boil until the sauce is transparent and thick. If it's too thick add more water, 1 tablespoon at a time.
5 Remove the ramekins from the oven and spread about 1 tablespoon of Mango Sauce on top of each custard. Serve the ramekins warm, chilled, or at room temperature.

Banana, Kiwi and Passion Fruit Salad

Chili sauce puts the "passion" in this banana, kiwi, and passion fruit salad. Although you may have never thought to toss your fruit salad with chili sauce, I will tell you that it's an amazing and exotic flavor experience—spicy, sweet, tart and perfectly punctuated with refreshing mint leaves.

SERVES 6
PREPARATION TIME: 15 MINUTES

4 ripe kiwis, peeled and quartered
    lengthwise
½ pound (250 g) fresh pineapple,
    peeled, cored and cut into ¼ in (6
    mm) pieces
1 passion fruit

DRESSING
4 tablespoons finely chopped fresh
    mint leaves
3 tablespoons freshly squeezed lime
    juice
1 tablespoon Asian chili sauce, prefer-
    ably Sriracha
1 tablespoon palm or brown sugar
2 ripe bananas, cut into ¼ in (6 mm)
    slices

1 Dressing: Whisk together mint leaves, lime juice, chili sauce, and palm sugar in a small bowl. Set aside.
2 Combine the bananas, kiwi, and passion fruit in a medium bowl.
3 Scoop out the passion fruit and add the seeds and juice to the bananas, kiwi fruit, and pineapple. Toss to combine and serve immediately.

COOK'S NOTE: When you buy passion fruit, look for a crinkled skin, which is a sign of ripeness.

Sweet, Ripe Mango with Sticky Rice

This dessert is sleek and elegant and the perfect ending to a Thai feast. Every time I make this sublime Thai favorite, the combination of refreshing mango, zesty mint, and warm sticky rice transports me right back to Railey Beach in Krabi where we'd enjoy this dessert in our beach cabana listening to only to the sounds of crashing waves.

MAKES 4 SERVINGS
PREPARATION TIME: 5 MINUTES + SOAKING TIME
COOKING TIME: 30 MINUTES

1 cup (225 g) uncooked Thai white or black sticky rice, soaked overnight, rinsed and drained
¼ teaspoon salt
2 cups (500 ml) water
½ vanilla bean
½ cup (85 g) packed palm or brown sugar
⅛ teaspoon salt
One 14 oz (400 ml) can coconut milk
4 small ripe mangos, sliced
Fresh mint leaves for garnish
Toasted black sesame seeds for garnish

1 Bring the sticky rice, salt, and 2 cups water to a boil in a medium saucepan. Reduce the heat to a simmer until the water evaporates, about 20 minutes. Remove from the heat and let it sit for 10 minutes. Transfer to a bowl.
2 Meanwhile, scrape the seeds from the vanilla bean and place them in a medium saucepan. Stir in the palm sugar, salt, and coconut milk. Heat over medium-low heat, stirring to dissolve the sugar, until steaming. Remove from the heat. Discard the vanilla pod.
3 Pour 1 cup (250 ml) of the coconut milk mixture over rice and stir to combine. Let stand for 30 minutes to blend the flavors.
4 Place a scoop of sticky rice on a small plate and arrange mango slices alongside it. Garnish with mint leaves and sprinkle with sesame seeds. Serve with the remaining co-conut milk mixture in a small serving bowl.

Lemongrass Custard

This is a classic custard recipe infused with lemongrass and is nothing short of heaven. Sophisticated, yet mild and creamy laced with a citrusy aroma and lemony flavor from the lemongrass. When buying fresh lemongrass, look for stalks that are fragrant, tightly formed, and of a lemony-green color on the lower stalk and turning to a truer green at the end of the stalk.

MAKES 4 SERVINGS
PREPARATION TIME: 5 MINUTES
COOKING TIME: 40 MINUTES

1 cup (250 ml) whole milk
1 cup (250 ml) coconut milk
4 tablespoons minced lemongrass
6 egg yolks
½ cup (100 g) sugar
Powdered sugar for dusting
Fresh mint leaves for garnish

1 Preheat oven to 275°F (135°C).
2 Bring the milk, coconut milk, and lemongrass to a simmer over medium-low heat in a saucepan. Cover and let simmer for 15 minutes. Remove from heat.
3 In a mixing bowl, beat the egg yolks with the sugar until thick. Strain the milk mixture through a fine-mesh sieve, then slowly pour it into the egg yolks, whisking constantly.
4 Pour the mixture into the ramekins, filling each one ¾ full. Place ramekins in a flat-bottomed glass dish. Fill this dish part-way with boiling water (⅓ to ½ way up the side of the ramekins). Gently place the dish in the oven, being careful not to spill the water.
5 Bake for 20 minutes, or until the custard has set.
6 Serve the ramekins at warm, cold, or at room temperature. Dust with powdered sugar before serving and garnish with mint leaves.

COOK'S NOTE: For a crème brulee version of this recipe, refrigerate cooked custards for 2 hours or up to overnight. Sprinkle 2 teaspoons of sugar evenly over each custard. Working with 1 custard at a time, hold a cooking blowtorch, so that flame is 2 inches (5 cm) above surface. Heat the surface with a direct flame so that the sugar melts and browns, about 2 minutes. Refrigerate until the custards are firm again but the topping is still brittle, at least 2 hours but no longer than 4 hours so that the topping doesn't soften.

Coconut Cake with Mango Sauce

My pastry chef/instructor friend, Theresa Frederickson takes the cake! Not only has she done a stint at Spago, she bakes awesome cakes, including a giant Curious George cake she made for the twins' 3rd birthday party. I asked her for her coconut cake recipe. Moist and delicious, this cake is made with creamy coconut milk and is drizzled with a sweet and juicy mango sauce for just the right finish.

SERVES 6–8
PREPARATION TIME: 10 MINUTES
COOKING TIME: 50 MINUTES

1 cup (226 g) unsalted butter, room temperature
2 cups (400 g) sugar
3 cups (400 g) all-purpose flour, plus more for dusting
1 teaspoon salt
2 teaspoons baking powder
3 large eggs
1 teaspoon vanilla extract
1 teaspoon coconut extract
One 14 oz (400 ml) can coconut milk
Toasted shredded coconut for topping

MANGO SAUCE
1 cup (250 ml) puréed mango
½ cup (100 g) sugar
1 tablespoon all-purpose cornstarch
¾ cup (185 ml) water

1 Preheat oven to 350°F (175°C). Spray a bundt pan with nonstick baking spray and dust with flour. In a small bowl, whisk together the flour, salt, and baking powder.
2 Using a mixer, cream the butter and sugar together until light and fluffy, about 3 minutes. Beat in the eggs, 1 at a time. Once incorporated, add the extracts. Stir in the coconut milk alternating with the flour mixture and mix until smooth.
3 Pour the batter into the prepared pan and bake until the center is firm and the cake comes away from the sides of the pan, about 50 minutes.
4 Mango Sauce: Combine all of the ingredients for the sauce in a small saucepan. Whisk until lump free. Place over medium heat, stirring constantly. Bring to a boil until the sauce is transparent and thick. If it's too thick add more water, 1 tablespoon at a time. Remove from heat.
5 Cool cake 5 minutes before turning it out onto a rack. Let cool completely on the rack. Top with shredded coconut and drizzle the sauce over top before serving.

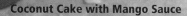
Coconut Cake with Mango Sauce

Coconut Thai Basil Ice Cream

I met Danielle Keene at a food and wine charity event, Cooking for Love, which I co-chair every year to benefit Break the Cycle. She's a super talented pastry chef and fun friend. She was also a finalist on Bravo TV's Top Chef Desserts and is owner of LA based Bittersweet Treats. She was kind of enough to share her delectable Coconut Thai Basil Ice Cream recipe with us. Smooth, creamy, and infused with Thai basil, this ice cream is simply divine. A wonderful complement to a spicy Thai meal and, because it's scooped into coconut shells, it's super fun to serve. Sweet!

MAKES 6–8 SERVINGS
PREPARATION TIME: 10 MINUTES + STEEPING AND FREEZING TIME
COOKING TIME: 5 MINUTES

½ cup (125 ml) heavy cream
1 cup (250 ml) whole milk
One 14 oz (400 ml) can coconut milk
¾ cup (50 g) sugar
¼ cup (5 g) fresh Thai or Italian basil leaves
6 egg yolks

3–4 whole coconuts
Fresh mint leaves for garnish

1 Bring the heavy cream, milk, coconut milk, and sugar in a medium saucepan to a simmer over medium-low heat. Remove from the heat and add the basil leaves. Cover with plastic wrap and allow to steep for 1 hour.
2 Remove the plastic wrap and return the mixture to a simmer. Transfer the mixture to a bowl containing the egg yolks and slowly whisk it. Strain, pressing the leaves with a spatula, and chill until the mixture is very cold, at least 2 hours (up to overnight). Spin in an ice cream maker according to manufacturer's instructions. Place it in a covered container and freeze until solid.
3 Cut the coconuts in half. Scoop the ice cream into the coconut shells. Garnish with mint leaves and serve immediately.

COOK'S NOTE: Look for coconuts at your grocery store which are pre-scored because they're easier to cut in half.

Thai Basil Lemon Soda

I felt like a true mixologist when my friend, Bill Tocantins of Elixir G, gave me a muddler as a gift. This recipe is a breeze, muddler or no muddler (a simple wooden spoon will do the trick). Thai Basil Lemon Soda is so refreshing and simple, I could sip it all day.

MAKES 4 SERVINGS
PREPARATION TIME: 10 MINUTES

½ **cup (125 ml) freshly squeezed lemon juice**
¼ **cup (50 g) sugar**
20 fresh Thai or Italian basil leaves
⅛ **teaspoon salt**
1 quart (1 liter) club soda

In a pitcher, add the lemon juice, sugar, basil leaves, and salt. Muddle ingredients with a muddler or the handle of a wooden spoon until the sugar dissolves. Add the ice and club soda and let sit until chilled. Strain into four 8 ounce (250 ml) glasses filled with ice. Garnish with lemon slices and serve.

COOK'S NOTE: For an adult treat, Thai this on for size: blend Thai basil lemon soda with crushed ice and vodka in blender. Enjoy!

Mango Shake

Shake it don't break it! In Thailand, mango shakes are enjoyed all over but usually consist simply of puréed mango blended with ice. This is a creamier version made with a bit of honey water and healthy coconut milk. I love to drink this chilled shake while having a spicy curry dish, like Phuket Chicken with Lemongrass Curry (page 72) to cool down my palate.

SERVES 2
PREPARATION TIME: 5 MINUTES

1 banana, cut into chunks
1 cup (200 g) frozen mango chunks
¼ **cup (65 ml) honey water (2 tablespoons honey**
    mixed with ¼ cup/65 ml hot water)
1 cup (250 ml) coconut milk
1 cup (175 g) ice
Fresh mint leaves for garnish

Place all the ingredients in a blender and blend until the ice is crushed and smooth. Garnish with mint leaves and serve immediately.

Thai Iced Tea

Thai iced tea is a popular drink served at Thai restaurants everywhere. The signature orange color comes from Thai tea leaves which you can find at a Thai market. If you can't find Thai tea, then black tea is a fine substitute. It's sweet, creamy, refreshing and a bit addicting (okay, more than a bit). Thai people like to top their Thai iced tea with a bit of evaporated milk for added creaminess and texture.

MAKES 4 SERVINGS
PREPARATION TIME: 5 MINUTES + STEEPING TIME
COOKING TIME: 10 MINUTES

1 quart (1 liter) boiling water
⅓ cup (66 g) sugar
6 Thai or black tea bags
2 star anise
½ cup (125 ml) sweetened condensed milk
½ cup (125 ml) evaporated milk

1 Bring 4 cups (1 liter) water to a boil. Add the sugar and stir until dissolved. Remove from heat. Steep the tea bags and star anise in the hot water for five minutes. Strain the tea bags and star anise from the liquid.
2 Add the condensed milk and stir to combine. Allow to cool to room temperature.
3 Fill four 8 ounce (250 ml) glasses with ice. Pour tea mixture into glasses leaving enough room for evaporated milk. Top each glass with 2 tablespoons each of evaporated milk.

Lemongrass Ginger Ale

There's nothing like a big, tall glass of ginger ale on a hot summer day. Here's a unique Southeast Asian twist on an old-fashioned favorite. This Lemongrass Ginger Ale makes the yummiest float with a couple of scoops of Coconut Thai Basil Ice Cream (page 134). I'd say this is definitely *not* your father's ginger ale.

MAKES 4 SERVINGS
PREPARATION TIME: 10 MINUTES + STEEPING TIME
COOKING TIME: 50 MINUTES

¾ cup (75 g) peeled and minced fresh ginger
¾ cup (75 g) minced lemongrass
2 cups (500 ml) water
¾ cup (150 g) sugar
Pinch of salt
1 quart (1 liter) club soda
3 tablespoons freshly squeezed lime juice
Fresh mint leaves for garnish

1 Bring the ginger, lemongrass, and water to a gentle boil over medium heat in a small saucepan. Reduce the heat immediately to medium-low and simmer partially covered, for 45 minutes. Remove from the heat and let steep, covered, for 20 minutes.
2 Strain the mixture through a sieve into a bowl, pressing on the ginger and lemongrass. Discard the ginger and lemongrass. Return the liquid to the saucepan and add sugar and salt. Heat over medium heat, stirring, until the sugar is dissolved. Chill the syrup in a covered jar in the refrigerator until cold.
3 Mix the ginger lemongrass syrup with club soda and lime juice. Fill four 8 ounce high ball glasses with ice and pour the ginger ale into the glasses. Garnish with mint leaves and serve.

Banana Spring Rolls

This is a crisp, sweet and light popular Thai dessert. It couldn't be easier to make and is always a favorite at my dinner parties. The hint of lemongrass in the chocolate sauce is divine and gives this sauce an exotic and aromatic verve.

MAKES 4 SERVINGS
PREPARATION TIME: 10 MINUTES
COOKING TIME: 22 MINUTES

4 spring roll wrappers
4 bananas
Lemon juice
Water
Oil for deep-frying
Powdered sugar for dusting
Fresh mint leaves for garnish

CHOCOLATE LEMONGRASS SAUCE
1 cup (250 ml) coconut milk
3 tablespoons palm or brown sugar
4 tablespoons minced lemongrass
6 oz (175 g) semisweet chocolate, chopped or semisweet chocolate chips

1 Chocolate Lemongrass Sauce: Bring the coconut milk, palm sugar, and lemongrass to a gentle boil in a small saucepan over medium heat, stirring to dissolve the palm sugar. Reduce the heat to medium-low and simmer, covered, for 15 minutes. Strain the mixture through a fine-mesh sieve. Return the mixture to the saucepan and stir in the chocolate. Bring to a simmer over medium-low heat and stir continuously until the chocolate melts. Remove from the heat.

2 Separate the spring roll wrappers and place them under a damp towel. Peel the bananas and slice each banana into three pieces. Coat the banana pieces with a little lemon juice. Place the banana pieces in a straight line in the bottom third of a spring roll wrapper.

3 Start rolling the spring roll wrapper tightly, folding in the edges as you go along to form a uniform spring roll. Seal the last tip with a little water. Repeat with the other bananas and store in the refrigerator until needed.

4 In a wok or deep skillet heat 2–3 inches (5–7.5 cm) of the oil to 350°F (175°C). Deep-fry the spring rolls until golden brown, about 30 seconds to 1 minute, turning frequently. Place on a wire rack to cool. Cut each spring roll in half (at an angle), place on a plate and dust with powdered sugar. Drizzle with warm Chocolate Lemongrass Sauce and garnish with mint leaves. Serve immediately.

How to Make Banana Spring Rolls

1 Combine the sauce ingredients in a small saucepan.

2 Bring the sauce to a gentle boil while stirring and then simmer.

3 Place banana pieces in a straight line in the bottom third of the spring roll wrapper.

4 Start rolling the spring roll wrapper tightly, folding in the edges as you go along to form a uniform spring roll.

5 Continue rolling to the top and seal the last tip with a little water.

6 Heat oil to 350°F (175°C) and fry the spring rolls a few at a time until golden brown, about 30 seconds to 1 minute.

Resources

On-line resources for Thai Ingredients:

Today, you can find the staple Thai ingredients you need at your local grocery store and an occasional trip to your local Asian market. If you don't live near an Asian market or it's just more convenient to have yellow soy bean sauce or roasted red chili paste arrive at your doorstep, luckily there are numerous on-line resources available. I've also included resources for Thai cooking tools and specialty products. Some of these on-line resources offer Asian and Thai-inspired dishware and tableware to enhance your Thai dining experience.

Thai Kitchen
www.thaikitchen.com

Temple of Thai
www.templeofthai.com

Amazon
www.amazon.com

Import Food
www.importfood.com

Grocery Thai
www.grocerythai.com

Asian Food Grocer
www.asianfoodgrocer.com

Adriana's Caravan
www.adrianascaravan.com

efooddepot.com
www.efooddepot.com

Red Boat Fish Sauce
www.redboatfishsauce.com

On-line resources for Thai Cooking Tools and Specialty Products:

Gourmet Sleuth
www.gourmetsleuth.com

The Wok Shop
www.thewokshop.com

Wok Star
www.wokstar.us

Sur La Table
www.surlatable.com

World Market
www.worldmarket.com

Cooking.com
www.cooking.com

Williams Sonoma
www.williamssonoma.com

Pier One
www.pierone.com

Thai Recipe Blogs:

Once you master the fundamental techniques in Thai cooking, you can gain further inspiration and feel armed to improvise and create your own Thai masterpieces. Here's a collection of my favorite Thai food blogs which feature some incredible and authentic recipes.

Enjoy Thai Food
www.enjoythaifood.com

Thai Food Master
www.thaifoodmaster.com

Rasa Malaysia
www.rasamalaysia.com

Chez Pim
www.chezpim.com

Thai Cooking with Jam
www.thaicookingwithjam.com

Bangkok Food Glutton
www.bangkokfoodglutton.com

Steamy Kitchen
www.steamykitchen.com

Riya's Kitchen
www.riya-kitchen.blogspot.com

Appon's Thai Food
www.khiewchanta.com

Joy's Thai Food
www.joysthaifood.com

She Simmers
www.shesimmers.com

Siam Food
www.siam-food-com.blogspot.com

Thai Cookbooks

There are some amazing Thai and Southeast Asian cookbooks out there. Here's a list of my favorites that I admire not only for providing such comprehensive backgrounds on Thai cooking but for their authentic recipes and stunning photography in many cases.

Easy Thai Cooking by Robert Danhi

Hot Sour Salty Sweet: A Culinary Journey through Southeast Asia by Jeffrey Alfrod and Namoi Duguid

Real Thai: The Best of Thailand's Regional Cooking by Nancie McDermott

Quick and Easy Thai by Nancie McDermott

The Best of Vietnamese and Thai Cooking by Mai Pham

Thai Street Food by David Thompson

Modern Thai Food by Martin Boetz

Index

Acknowledgments

I feel so grateful and blessed to have been given the opportunity to create this book. I always dreamed of bringing my passion for Thai food to life using my voice and through gorgeous photography. When I met Christopher Johns from Tuttle Publishing at the International Association of Culinary Professionals (IACP) Conference it was the start of a dream come true and I am so honored to be part of the Tuttle family.

I started my food blog, The Sweet and Sour Chronicles (http://www.thesweetandsourchronicles.com) at the urging of so many people like me who juggle a million things at once and still manage to get dinner on the table for their families. What I realized was that while everyone loves Thai food there aren't many resources out there to translate authentic Thai recipes for the everyday home cook.

Like raising a child, writing a cookbook takes a village. I could never have written this book without the love and support of my friends and family. First and foremost, I'd like to thank my husband and best friend, Matthew. Not only was he subjected to a round-the-clock Thai test kitchen, he gave me invaluable advice and challenged me to make the book as great as it could be. I also want to thank my stepdaughter Kyla and twins, Dylan and Becca, for their patience and understanding. Many thanks to our au pairs, Julia Franzen and Jessica Cousins, who came to the rescue and kept our family on its schedule despite a stream of testers coming in and out of our kitchen. I'd like to give thanks to Delfina Garcia for cleaning up from the aftermath of a week's worth of testing.

This book would have never seen the light of day without the amazing support of my talented sous chef, Stacy Mears. She worked tirelessly throughout the entire process and never complained once (and actually talked me down from the ledge at least twice). I have to thank her husband, Mark Mears and her daughters, Brianna and McKenna, for letting me borrow her for so many hours!

I am so grateful for the support of my dear friend and former editor, Katie Workman, who provided the foreword despite being in the middle of her own cookbook launch (The Mom 100 is awesome…go buy it).

I am humbled by the quotes given by Michael Chiarello, Susan Feniger, Christos Garkinos, Jaden Hair, Brad Johnson, Bee Yinn Low, Jeannie Mai, Iron Chef Morimoto, Roy Yamaguchi, Master Chef Martin Yan, and Andrew Zimmern. Thank you so much. For those of you I mentioned who knew my amazing mother, Chef Leeann Chin, I hope you feel I did her proud.

Many thanks to Theresa Frederickson, Danielle Keene, Chef Mohan and Chef Hong Thaimee for sharing delicious recipes from their personal vaults for the book.

I have to give a million thanks to my testers who dove into each recipe with passion and honest feedback:

-Bill Chin
-Jean Chin
-Laura Chin
-Adam Drucker
-Steven Durbahn
-Theresa Frederickson
-Neil Newman
-Stacy Mears
-Cathy Miltenberger

I'd like to thank some of my amazing friends for their endless support: Bob Bell, Carol Cheng-Mayer, Traci Ching, Diana Choi, Dan Davis, Anne Deloia, Rita Drucker, Marissa Durazzo, Sabrina Ironside, Jeffrey Kasanoff, Allie Korosi, Melanie Kosaka, Frank Lomento, Patrick Martin, Catherine McCord, JJ McKay, Carla Moreira, Kristin Nicholas, Marty Ordman, Steve Patscheck, Hugo Rojas, Rich Ross, Amy Rosskelley, Mary Sadeghy, Adam Sanderson, Valerie Shavers, Randi Spieker, Sven Spieker, Terry Stanley, Mark Stone, Michael Stone and Mary Wagstaff. From letting me camp out in their midtown apartment (you know who you are) so I could meet my deadline to serving as guinea pigs while I unveiled new recipes, I am so lucky to have you in my life.

To my wonderful agents, Sally Ekus and Lisa Ekus: Thanks for always believing in me and my vision.

I am indebted to the team at Tuttle for working so hard to make this book a reality. Thank you to my editor, Bud Sperry, Christopher Johns, Rowan Muelling-Auer, photographer Masano Kawana, June Chong, Chan Sow Yun and Victor Mingovits.

If I've left anyone out, I'm so sorry for the omission.

Many thanks to you all and Happy Cooking!

Published by Tuttle Publishing, an imprint of Periplus Editions (HK) Ltd.

www.tuttlepublishing.com

Photos used in endpapers: © Giuliachristin/Dreamstime.com; © Junk-girl/Dreamstime.com; © Combodesign/Dreamstime.com; © Chanoey-chanchao/Dreamstime.com; © Charlieedward/Dreamstime.com; © Edwardkaraa/Dreamstime.com; © Thanamat/Dreamstime.com; © Minyun9260/Dreamstime.com; © Oatmax/Dreamstime.com

Pattern background: © Stockerman/Dreamstime.com; © Eyen120819/Dreamstime.com; © Toa555/Dreamstime.com; © Wiangya/Dreamstime.com; © Rprongjai/Dreamstime.com; © Anankkml/Dreamstime.com; © Rutchapong/Dreamstime.com; © Worachet Denyuk/123rf.com; © Rin Boonprasan/123rf.com; © Sujin Jetkasettakorn/123rf.com; © Kanlayar Sanwisat/123rf.com; © krisckam/123rf.com

Library of Congress Cataloging-in-Publication Data in process

ISBN 978-0-8048-4371-3

Distributed by
North America, Latin America & Europe
Tuttle Publishing
364 Innovation Drive
North Clarendon, VT 05759-9436 U.S.A.
Tel: 1 (802) 773-8930; Fax: 1 (802) 773-6993
info@tuttlepublishing.com; www.tuttlepublishing.com

Japan
Tuttle Publishing
Yaekari Building, 3rd Floor, 5-4-12 Osaki,
Shinagawa-ku, Tokyo 141-0032
Tel: (81) 3 5437-0171; Fax: (81) 3 5437-0755
sales@tuttle.co.jp; www.tuttle.co.jp

Asia Pacific
Berkeley Books Pte. Ltd
61 Tai Seng Avenue, #02-12, Singapore 534167
Tel: (65) 6280-1330; Fax: (65) 6280-6290
inquiries@periplus.com.sg; www.periplus.com

Printed in Singapore   1304CP
16 15 14 13   10 9 8 7 6 5 4 3 2 1

The Tuttle Story
"Books to Span the East and West"

Most people are surprised to learn that the world's largest publisher of books on Asia had its humble beginnings in the tiny American state of Vermont. The company's founder, Charles Tuttle, came from a New England family steeped in publishing, and his first love was books—especially old and rare editions.

Tuttle's father was a noted antiquarian dealer in Rutland, Vermont. Young Charles honed his knowledge of the trade working in the family bookstore, and later in the rare books section of Columbia University Library. His passion for beautiful books—old and new—never wavered throughout his long career as a bookseller and publisher.

After graduating from Harvard, Tuttle enlisted in the military and in 1945 was sent to Tokyo to work on General Douglas MacArthur's staff. He was tasked with helping to revive the Japanese publishing industry, which had been utterly devastated by the war. When his tour of duty was completed, he left the military, married a talented and beautiful singer, Reiko Chiba, and in 1948 began several successful business ventures.

To his astonishment, Tuttle discovered that post- war Tokyo was actually a book-lover's paradise. He befriended dealers in the Kanda district and began supplying rare Japanese editions to American libraries. He also imported American books to sell to the thousands of GIs stationed in Japan. By 1949, Tuttle's business was thriving, and he opened Tokyo's very first English-language bookstore in the Takashi-maya Department Store in Ginza, to great success. Two years later, he began publishing books to fulfill the growing interest of foreigners in all things Asian.

Though a westerner, Tuttle was hugely instrumental in bringing a knowledge of Japan and Asia to a world hungry for information about the East. By the time of his death in 1993, he had published over 6,000 books on Asian culture, history and art—a legacy honored by Emperor Hirohito in 1983 with the "Order of the Sacred Treasure," the highest honor Japan bestows upon non-Japanese.

The Tuttle company today maintains an active backlist of some 1,500 titles, many of which have been continuously in print since the 1950s and 1960s—a great testament to Charles Tuttle's skill as a publisher. More than 60 years after its founding, Tuttle Publishing is more active today than at any time in its history, still inspired by Charles Tuttle's core mission—to publish fine books to span the East and West and provide a greater understanding of each.